The New Foundling Hospital For Wit

Foundling hospital

THE

NEW FOUNDLING HOSPITAL

FOR

W I T.

BEING A COLLECTION OF

FUGITIVE PIECES, IN PROSE AND VERSE,

NOT IN ANY OTHER COLLECTION.

WITH

SEVERAL PIECES NEVER BEFORE PUBLISHED.

A NEW EDITION,

CORRECTED, AND CONSIDERABLY ENLARGED.

IN SIX VOLUMES.

VOL. VI.

LONDON:

PRINTED FOR J. DEBRETT, OPPOSITE BURLING-
TON-HOUSE, PICCADILLY.

M DCC LXXXVI.

Contents to the Sixth Volume.

VOL. VI.

THE

NEW FOUNDLING HOSPITAL

FOR

W   I   T.

EPITAPH

ON THE DEATH OF A VERY YOUNG LADY.

BY BRIAN EDWARDS, ESQ.

SCARCE had the tender hand of Time
   Maria's bloom brought forth,
Nor yet advanc'd to Beauty's prime,
   Tho' ripe in Beauty's worth :

When Fate untimely feal'd her doom,
   And fhew'd, in one fhort hour,
A lovely fky, an envious gloom,
   A rainbow and a fhow'r.

       WRITTEN

WRITTEN ON A WINDOW AT AN INN, UNDER SOME INFAMOUS VERSES.

BY THE SAME.

WHEN Dryden's clown, unknowing what he
      fought,
His hours in whiftling fpent, for want of thought,
The guiltlefs Oaf his vacancy of fenfe
Supplied, and amply too, by innocence.
Did modern fwains, poffefs'd of Cymon's pow'rs,
In Cymon's manner wafte there weary hours,
Th' indignant trav'ller would not blufhing fee
This chryftal pane difgrac'd by infamy!
   Severe the fate of modern fools, alas!
When Vice and Folly mark them as they pafs:
Like pois'nous vermin o'er the whiten'd wall,
The filth they leave--ftill points out where they crawl!

EPIGRAM.

BY THE SAME.

POET, faid Chloe, with a laugh,
Your Mufe fhall write my epitaph.
If, tombftone-like, my lovely maid,
I were on that foft bofom laid,
Fond love fhould write, if you fhould die,
Both epitaph and elegy.

ON

ON THE DEATH OF GENERAL MONTGOMERY.

BY THE SAME.

MONTGOMERY falls ! let no fond breaſt repine,
That Hampden's glorious death, brave chief, was
    thine,
With his ſhall Freedom conſecrate thy name ;
Shall date her riſing glories from thy fame ;
Shall build her throne of empire on thy grave :
What nobler fate can patriot virtues crave !

ODE FOR THE NEW YEAR.

BY THE SAME.

Prob Curia inverſique mores !   HOR.

GENIUS of Albion ! whither art thou fled !
Thou, who waſt wont at Freedom's call to riſe,
  With thund'ring voice, and heav'n-directed eyes,
And mock th' oppreſſor's rage, or ſmite the tyrant
    dead !
    O ſtretch again thy ſaving hand,
      In mercy to this groaning iſle !
    No common ills thine aid demand ;
      Corruption triumphs in her ſpoil ;
    Fierce Diſcord hurls her torch on high ;
    Nor public weal, nor ſocial tie

       Can

Can fix the fordid, felfifh mind:
Ambition breaks Law's feeble chain,
Swol'n Lux'ry leads her bloated train,
And Ruin ftalks behind!

II.

Beyond the rough Atlantic tide,
Infpir'd by Virtue and by Thee,
Thy junior fons ftill dare be free;—
Nor e'er fhall fubtle fraud divide
The gen'rous band. Oh! while the tempeft low'rs,
Reflect our caufe is one—that Freedom's foes are ours!

III.

Peace to thy fhade, lamented King;
Great Brunfwick, fecond of thy race,
Call'd England's happy throne to grace,
What time fair Freedom made each valley ring.
From the cold tomb could'ft thou arife,
How would this profpect fear thine eyes,
And drive thee back in wild affright!
For lo! fierce iffuing from their native north,
The howling furies murd'rous ftorms fend forth;
Glut the Gaul's proud revenge, and fpread vile
Slav'ry's night!

IV. In

IV.

In vain, alas ! thy gallant son,
  On fam'd Culloden's glorious field,
   Taught the proud trait'rous Scot to yield,
And deathless laurels nobly won.
In vain rejoic'd th' admiring world,
  When our brave fires, by Naſſau led,
At tyrant-pow'r their thunders hurl'd
  While the dark tyrant crouch'd and fled.
No longer now, in patriot ſhackles bound,
With fruitleſs wailing Envy bites her chain ;
Oppreſſion leaps o'er Freedom's ſacred mound,
And vainly Hampden fought, and Sydney bled in vain !

V.

Lo ! Saunders mingles with the mighty dead ;
  No more th' avenger of his country's wrong :
O'er his cold duſt let no weak tear be ſhed ;
  He wept, alas ! that he had liv'd too long.
O greatly glorious ! had he died
   Ere ſet in darkneſs Britain's ſun ;
Ere frantic rage and Stuart pride,
   That empire loſt his valour won !
" What more, he cried, can adverſe fate require ?"
Dying he ſaw his country's fame expire ;
Saw her bright croſs he late triumphant ſpread,
Droop on the ſick'ning gale, and bluſh with deeper red !

VI.

Hark! thro' America's indignant shore,
What groans for vengeance rend th' affrighted skies!
Foul impious War hath broken Nature's ties;
  And Britain, terror of the world no more,
  Turns on herself, and drinks her children's gore!
Oh! quickly drop the murd'rous sword,
  What horrors rise around?
Can'st thou, ill-fated realm, afford
  With thine own blood to drench the ground.
The vet'ran, yet untaught to yield,
Reluctant views the death-fraught field,
Conscious of guilt would fain retreat,
And dreads ev'n vict'ry as defeat;—
In vain: still o'er Ontario's flood.
With ghastly smile, and blasting eyes,
Stern Alva's guilty spirit flies,
And snuffs the scented air, and rages still for blood!

VII.

Hear how her sons Iberia tells
  Exulting as the tempest swells;
And faithless Gallia, with prophetic eye,
Beholds thy golden streams of Commerce dry,
Or marks them for her own. " O great event,"
She cries,—" Thy shame and punishment,
                              " Rash

" Rafh, ruin'd rival! Now I fee
" Thy palm of glory fnatch'd by me ;
" That envied prize *, by Nature giv'n,
" Which rais'd thy tow'ring front to Heav'n,
" Spurn'd by thyfelf!—Oh! fpeed thy ling'ring fate,
" And to thyfelf be falfe,--to make my empire great!"

VIII.

But Britain, happier fates are thine :
Thy fun fhall yet unclouded fhine!
A day (nor far remote) fhall come,
When, Rage difarm'd, and Envy dumb,
The pious child, her forrows o'er,
Shall urge the loud complaint no more :
But nourifh (in her fuff'ring bleft)
Th' expiring parent, from her breaft!
For lo! Futurity her page unfolds :
What floods of glory fill yon weftern fkies!
I fee, I fee, the radiant forms arife,
Where venerable Time fair Truth upholds,
And awful Juftice, her divine compeer,
Exalts her gen'rous brow, and fhakes her glitt'ring
    fpear !

* Commerce.

IX. " Ye

IX.

" Ye parricides, who broke the golden cords
  " Of filial piety—maternal love ;
" Ye perjur'd fenators—ye venal lords,
   " Now curfe your damned deeds—for vengeance
      " dwells with Jove !
      " America, no longer thou
" Shalt lift thy plaintive voice in vain ;
      " Nor Britain's fons to flav'ry bow,
      " Nor forge for others necks the chain !
      " 'Tis Juftice fpeaks !" above controul,
Her thunders fmite the guilty foul.
See murder'd Sydney grimly fmile,
And virtuous Ruffel blefs her glorious toil !
Oh fleep, ye facred fhades! in endlefs reft ;
The fign of Mercy, beaming from the weft,
Kind Heav'n has giv'n ;—for o'er the patriot crowd
Bright Conqueft foars aloft--and claps her wings aloud.

STANZAS

STANZAS

OCCASIONED BY THE DEATH OF ALICO, AN AFRI-
CAN SLAVE, CONDEMNED FOR REBELLION IN
JAMAICA, 1765.

[☞ He is fuppofed to addrefs his Wife at the place
of Execution.]

BY THE SAME.

I.

'TIS paft :—Ah ! calm thy cares to reft !
    Firm and unmov'd am I :—
In Freedom's caufe I bar'd my breaft,—
    In Freedom's caufe I die.

II.

Ah ftop ! thou do'ft me fatal wrong :—
    Nature will yet rebel :
For I have lov'd thee very long,
    And lov'd thee very well.

III.

To native fkies and peaceful bow'rs,
    I foon fhall wing my way ;
Where joy fhall lead the circling hours,
    Unlefs too long thy ftay,

B 5   IV. Oh

IV.

Oh fpeed, fair fun ! thy courfe divine ;
 My Abala remove ;—
There thy bright beams fhall ever fhine,
 And I for ever love !

V.

On thofe bleft fhores—a Slave no more !
 In peaceful eafe I'll ftray ;
Or roufe to chace the mountain boar,
 As unconfin'd as day !

VI.

No Chriftian tyrant there is known
 To mark his fteps with blood,
Nor fable Mis'ry's piercing moan
 Refounds thro' ev'ry wood.

VII.

Yet have I heard the melting tongue,
 Have feen the falling tear ;
Known the good heart by pity wrung,
 Ah ! that fuch hearts are rare !

VIII. Now,

VIII.

Now, Chriftian, glut thy ravifh'd eyes
—I reach the joyful hour;
Now bid the fcorching flames arife,
And thefe poor limbs devour:

IX.

But know, pale Tyrant, 'tis not thine
Eternal war to wage;
The death thou giv'ft fhall but combine
To mock thy baffled rage.

X.

O Death, how welcome to th' oppreft!
Thy kind embrace I crave:
Thou bring'ft to Mis'ry's bofom reft,
And *Freedom to the Slave.*

ON READING BOLINGBROKE'S REFLECTIONS ON THE CHARACTER OF POPE.

BY THE SAME.

SOFT be thy fleep, ill-fated bard!
Thy virtue is thy fole reward.
Alas! the lov'd, fweet voice of Fame
Is Folly;—Friendfhip but a name!

B 6

Injurious

Injurious meed! O'er him, whose eye,
As light'ning keen, made Dulness fly,
Ere yet was broke life's golden chain;——
(Blest fav'rite in the Muses' train!)
Shall Dulness *now* presume to tread,
And Envy mark him out when dead!

Curst be the vain, false, coward slave,
Who thus aims vengeance on the grave;
Thus breaks thro' Friendship's sacred laws;——
——What satire, Pope, is thy applause!*

TO LADY BOYNTON, CUTTING HER NAME IN TH BARK OF A TREE.

BY SIR GRIFFITH BOYNTON.

TO pensive minds superior truth belong,
Whose sacred precepts form the voice of song:
They with soft Solitude sweet converse hold,
And love the whisper'd tale by Fancy told.

While on this stem, (now consecrate to Fame)
Thou giv'st to future years the darling name,
What crowding thoughts within my bosom move,
Swell at my heart, and wake each sense of love!

* Alluding to the conclusion of his Essay on Man.

This

This plant thy Damon, in life's fragrant morn,
With foſt'ring hand ſelected from the thorn;
Faſt, with his years, the ſhooting ſcion grew,
Nor mark'd the varied ſeaſons as they flew;
Together paſs'd with Time his ample round:
(Hark! as you write, he gives the boding ſound)
His * " creeping hours," in myſtic days of yore,
Tun'd the ſweed reed on Avon's fairy ſhore:
Then ill-rewarded worth, or fruitleſs love,
Sought, and found ſolace in the lonely grove;
From prying eyes a willing exile ran,
And all th' obtruſive intercourſe of man.

Revolve the paſt, we paint the coming years;
The garlands Fancy wove Reflection tears;
There roſeate bloſſom moans its balmy prime,
Borne on the fleeting wing of ruthleſs Time:
Beauty awaits its all-involving gloom,
Nor chears the wintry frown that ſhades the tomb:
Yet be it mine, by Truth and Beauty fir'd,
To praiſe thoſe charms which Lyttleton admir'd.

* Shakeſpeare. As You Like It.

VERSES

VERSES

WRITTEN IN A COTTAGE AT PARK-PLACE, THE
SEAT OF THE RIGHT HONOURABLE GENERAL
CONWAY.

BY THE REVEREND MR. POWYS.

THE works of Art let others praife,
Where Pride her wafte of wealth betrays,
And Fafhion, independent grown,
Ufurps her parent Nature's throne,
Lays all her fair dominions wafte,
And calls the devaftation Tafte.
But I—who ne'er, with fervile awe,
Give Fafhion's whims the force of law,
Scorn all the glitter of expence,
When deftitute of ufe and fenfe.
More pleas'd to fee the wanton rill,
Which trickles from fome craggy hill,
Free thro' the valley wind its way,
Than when, immur'd in walls of clay,
It ftrives in vain its bonds to break,
And ftagnates in a crooked lake.
With fighs I fee the native oak
Bow to th' inexorable ftroke,
Whilft an exotic puny race
Of upftart fhrubs ufurps its place,

Which,

Which, born beneath a milder sky,
Shrink at a wintry blast, and die.
I ne'er behold without a smile
The venerable Gothic pile,
Which in our fathers' wiser age
Was shelter'd from the tempest's rage,
Stand to the dreary north expos'd,
Within a Chinese fence inclos'd.

For me, each leaden God may reign
In quiet o'er his old domain;
Their claim is good by Poet's laws,
And Poets must support their cause.
But when old Neptune's fish-tail'd train
Of Tritons, haunts an upland plain;
When Dian seems to urge the chace,
In a snug garden's narrow space;
When Mars, with insult rude, invades
The virgin Muses' peaceful shades;
With light'ning arm'd, when angry Jove
Scares the poor tenants of the grove,
I cannot blindly league with those,
Who thus the Poet's creed oppose.
To Nature, in my earliest youth,
I vow'd my constancy and truth;
When in her * Hardwicke's much-lov'd shade
Enamour'd of her charms I stray'd:

* The Seat of P. Powys, Esq. in Oxfordshire.

And

And as I rov'd the woods among,
Her praise in lisping numbers sung:
Nor will I now resign my heart,
A captive to her rival art.
Far from the pageant scenes of pride,
She still my careless steps shall guide,
Whether by Contemplation led,
The rich romantic wilds I tread,
Where Nature, for her pupil man,
Has sketch'd out many a noble plan;
Or whether from yon wood crown'd brow,
I view the lovely vale below.
For when, with more than common care,
Nature had sketch'd her landscape there,
Her Conway caught the fair design,
And soften'd ev'ry harsher line;
In pleasing lights each object plac'd,
And heighten'd all the piece with taste.
O Conway * ! whilst the public voice
Applauds our Sov'reign's well weigh'd choice,
Fain would my patriot Muse proclaim
The Statesman's and the Soldier's fame:
And bind immortal on thy brow
The civic crown and laurel bough.
But tho' unskill'd to join the choir,
Who aptly tune the courtly lyre,

* General Conway was at this time Secretary of State.

Tho'

Tho' with the vaffals of thy ftate,
I never at thy levee wait,
Yet be it oft my happier lot,
To meet thee in this rural cot,
To fee thee here thy mind unbend,
And quit the Statefman for the Friend:
Whilft fmiles unbought, and void of art,
Spring genuine from the focial heart.

Happy the Mufe, which here retir'd,
By gratitude like mine infpir'd;
Dupe to no party, loves to pay,
To worth like thine, her grateful lay:
And in no venal verfe commend,
The man of Tafte and Nature's friend.

ON BEING DESIRED BY LADY CAMDEN TO WRITE
VERSES ON BAYHAM ABBEY, THE SEAT OF JOHN
PRATT, ESQ. NEAR TUNBRIDGE WELLS,

BY THE SAME.

I.

DON'T you (cries Clio jeering) now,
Wifh to recall a certain vow,

Which

Which late you rashly made,
When, in a pettish mood, you swore
To leave off rhyming, and no more
  Invoke the Muse's aid ?

II.

When young, by tender tales of love
You wish'd young Celia's heart to move,
    And eager snatch'd the lyre,
Help me, some friendly Muse, you cried,
Oh deign my artless hand to guide,
    My fault'ring voice inspire.

III.

And when you strove in verse to raise
A trophy to your Conway's praise,
    His worth, his taste expressing ;
Again, a suppliant to the Nine,
I saw you bow before our shrine,
    Your languid pow'rs confessing.

IV.

But older now and wiser grown,
These vain connexions you disown,

Our

Our dictates you difclaim,
You fcorn the Mufes' idle crew,
You're bid them all a laft adieu,
 And hate a borrow'd name.

V.

Yet when in yon fequefter'd fcene,
With Contemplation's thoughtful mien,
 That hallow'd ground you trod,
Where cloifter'd monks with zeal infpir'd
Far from the bufy world retir'd,
 To folitude and God.

VI.

I heard your friends the lays demand,
I faw you take the pen in hand
 Impatient to comply:
I faw you rack your lab'ring brains,
To form the dull defcriptive ftrains,
 Whilft I ftood laughing by.

VII.

Fain would I fing (perplext you faid)
The lovely landfcape here difplay'd,

Which

Which charms each ravish'd fenfe;
The ruin'd Abbey's roofless iles,
And all the venerable fpoils
    Of funk magnificence.

VIII.

The verdant lawns, the wood-crown'd hills,
The limpid lakes, the bubbling rills,
    The lulling water-falls;
The flow'rs which blended odours fhed,
The robes of mantling ivy fpread
    Around the mould'ring walls.

IX.

Sweet fcenes! by Nature's pencil plann'd,
Retouch'd by Tafte's judicious hand,
    Without the glare of Art;
Tho' rafhly I've abjur'd the Mufe,
Can fhe, when fuch the theme, refufe
    Her influence to impart?

X.

Defponding thus did you lament,
But could you hope I would relent,

And favour your approaches ?
Nay, ceafe, unjuftly (I replied)
To tax me with contempt and pride,
And load me with reproaches.

XI.

Whene'er I bow'd before your fhrine,
You know that ev'ry pray'r of mine
In empty air was loft:
I never fought poetic fame,
Truth ever was my leading aim,
Sincerity my boaft.

XII.

But could I hope to gain from you
Thofe pow'rs, which mark the chofen few,
On whom you deign to fmile ;
Could I fuppofe you would infpire
My bofom with a Churchill's fire,
And elevate my ftile ?

XIII.

I'd fervently your aid implore;
I'd fcribble doggrel rhimes no more ;
But emulous of fame,
Would grateful join a nation's praife,
And decorate th' immortal lays
With Camden's honour'd name.

ON

ON the 10th of January, 1777, the Comedy of the Provok'd Hufband was acted, at a New Theatre, near Henley upon Thames, by the following perfons:

Lord Townly,	by	Lord Villiers.
Manly,	by	Mr. Milles.
Sir F. Wronghead	by	Mr. Putye.
Count Baffet,	by	Lord Malden.
'Squire Richard,	by	Hon. Mr. Onflow.
Moody,	by	Capt. Stewart.
Poundage and Conftable,	by }	Capt. Churchill.
Ld Townly's fervant	by	Mr. Tutridge.
Manly's fervant,	by	Mr. Hodges, jun.
Lady Townly,	by	Mifs Hodges.
Lady Grace	by	Mifs Clarke.
Lady Wronghead,	by	Mifs Hervey.
Mifs Jenny,	by	Mifs P. Hopkins.
Myrtilla,	by	Mifs Hopkins.
Mrs. Motherly,	by	Mrs. Johnfon.
Trufty,	by	Mifs Newhill.

UPON THIS OCCASION THE FOLLOWING PROLOGUE
WAS SPOKEN BY LORD VILLIERS.

MOST raw recruits, in times of Peace appear
To brave all dangers, and to mock at fear;
But when call'd forth to tread th' embattl'd plain,
They fairly wifh themfelves at home again.

Whilft

Whilſt hardy vet'rans, long inur'd to arms,
Hear, unappall'd, the battle's loud alarms.

Thus we, unpractis'd in the ſtage's arts,
Have, without fear, rehears'd our various parts,
Talk'd wond'rous big of our theatric feats,
And dar'd the ceuſures of the vacant ſeats.
But now, alas! the caſe is alter'd quite,
When ſuch an audience opens on the ſight;
Garrick himſelf, in ſuch a ſituation,
(Tho' ſure to pleaſe) might feel ſome palpitation.
Our anxious breaſts no ſuch preſumption cheers,
Light are our hopes, but weighty are our fears;
So (for 'tis now too late to quit the field)
We to your judgment at diſcretion yield;
O then be merciful: the fault's not ours,
If, with a wiſh to pleaſe, we want the pow'rs.

EPILOGUE,

WRITTEN BY MR. COLMAN, FOR LADY WRONG-
HEAD, AND ALTERED FOR MANLY.

SPOKEN BY MR. MILLES.

I FEAR the Ladies think my laſt night's dealing
Betray'd a heart quite deſtitute of feeling;

Who

Who to my married friends such lessons gave,
As make each husband think his wife a slave :
So, doctor-like, I took an early round,
And just step in to tell you that I found
My Lady Townly quite to health restor'd,
And cousin Wronghead's pulse is vastly lower'd ;
The first, whose bosom grateful Friendship warm'd,
Thus spoke the dictates of a heart reform'd :
" Sick of my follies, faithful to my vows *,
" I'm now re-married to my noble spouse ;
" Ladies there are at this may feel remorse,
" And find perhaps more charms in a divorce.
" I've trod the giddy round, and don't deplore,
" That the gay dream of dissipation's o'er :
" But Lady Wronghead still bewails her fate,
" And sighs for splendor, equipage and state.
" Farewel, dear scenes, she cried ; was ever wife,
" Born with a genius for the gayest life,
" Like me untimely blasted in her bloom—
" Like me condemn'd to such a dismal doom ?
" No London—when I just began to taste it ;
" No money—when I just knew how to waste it.
" Farewel--the high-plum'd head, the cushion'd tete,
" Which takes the cushion from its prop'rer seat.
" Seven is the main !—that sound must now expire,
" Lost at hot cockles, round a Christmas fire.

* The lines marked with inverted Commas were in the original.

" Farewel

" Farewel—dear fcenes, where late fuch joys I knew,
" Drefs, cards, and dice, I bid ye all adieu!
" Thofe joys thus vanifh'd, I fhall tafte no more,
" For Lady Wronghead's occupation's o'er.
" How fhall I drag out life, and how, alas!
" Shall tedious country winter evenings pafs."

Dear Ma'am, I faid, your groundlefs fears difmifs,
I have a thought—a new one—it is this:
Shall we come down, and try to act a play?
A play!—and what d'ye think the wits will fay?
" Unheard, with keeneft fatire they'll decry it,
" Turn all to farce, and fwear 'tis vain to try it."

Avaunt, fuch wits! who, with ill-judging fpleen,
Shall rudely ftrive to blaft the well-meant fcene.
Far happier he, his faults, like us, who ftops,
And checks his follies when the curtain drops,
No more in vice or error to engage,
And play the fool at large on life's great ftage.

[30]

PROLOGUE

TO THE FRENCH PIECE OF PYGMALION, PER-
FORMED BY MONSIEUR TESSIER.

SPOKEN BY LORD MALDEN.

As some there are who may not know the story,
Which the French Poet means to lay before ye,
I'll tell you in plain Englifh what he fays:

A young unmarried Prince, in former days,
Long rail'd at wedlock, but could never find
In all the fex a woman to his mind:
Some were too fhort, and others were too tall;
Too fat, too thin, there were fome fault in all.
Tir'd with the fruitlefs fearch, at length, he cried,
Art fhall fupply what Nature has denied;
I'll make a faultlefs maid. So faid, fo done,
Juft to his tafte he form'd a maid of ftone;
Th' enraptur'd artift as her charms he view'd,
Stood by the magic of his art fubdu'd:
But yet fhe was a piece of mere *ftill life,*
And fomething more he wanted in a wife.
A wife he thought fome little warmth fhould fhare,
(Are there none here whofe wives have fome to fpare?)
He kifs'd her oft; but, ah! how cold the kifs,
Efpecially in fuch a night as this.

Vain

Vain was his art, (for do whate'er he cou'd)
There was no comfort without flesh and blood:
To Venus he addrefs'd his fervent pray'r,
That fhe fhould animate the obd'rate fair;
For Venus can, whene'er fhe will, impart
A yielding foftnefs to the hardeft heart.
His pray'r was heard—to him fhe turn'd her head,
And o'er her limbs the glow of life was fpread:
Convinc'd at laft, he feels her pulfe beat high,
And wanton feem'd to roll her am'rous eye;
Loos'd was her tongue, fhe was indeed a wife,
And he no more complain'd *fhe wanted life.*

Lord Villiers admirably fupported the very difficult
character of Lord Townly, both as to voice, figure,
action, and elocution:—He was eafy, animated, and
graceful;—and perhaps the character never appeared
to more advantage in the hands of any performer,
except Mr. Barry. If any part of his performance
can be found fault with, he did not feem to exprefs
fufficient difpleafure in his countenance at his Lady's
conduct; but that is not to be wondered at, as Lady
Villiers never gives him reafon to practife it; and
without practife it was impoffible to be feigned, when
the enchanting Mifs Hodges, in the character of
Lady Townly, was fmiling before his eyes.

We beg both Meffrs. Yates and Macklin's pardon,
when we fay we prefer Mr. Fury to either of them for

a Sir

a Sir Francis Wronghead; and if he could be prevailed upon to appear on either of the London Theatres, we would advise the Managers to lose no time in striking a bargain with him.

Mr. Milles, who filled the part of Manly, we are told frequently treads the stage at North Aston; but he is more used to Tragedy than Comedy; it is a pity that the prompter did not put him in mind he was acting Comedy that night; but we have been informed, that office was filled by a reverend Divine, who possibly advised him to make so moral and so grave an appearance.

It is to be regretted, that Count Baffet was not acted by a person less delicate in his principles than Lord Malden; for it required one more hackneyed in the ways of the world, to do the Count that justice which Vanbrugh intended him: however, let us not forget to say, that Lord Malden was generally thought to act as well as any of them, when he made love to Miss Jenny.

'Squire Richard was so well performed by Mr. Onflow, that we really imagined Lord Villiers was so distressed for a gentleman performer, that he had been obliged to put up with one of his young tenants in the country. Mr. Onflow did so totally

divest

diveſt himſelf of his own character, and entered ſo thoroughly into that of 'Squire Richard.

Captain Stewart, in the part of honeſt John Moody, was humorous and characteriſtic; both his dreſs and addreſs were eaſy and natural: In ſhort, the Captain ſeemed to be perfectly at home in the character, though I ſuſpect, from his accent, that he was a little further north even than Yorkſhire. At the ſame time one would ſuppoſe, from his *en bon point*, that he was not quite ſo far as the Cave of Famine.

Mr. Hodges would have done Manly's ſervant better if he could have kept his gravity; but he unfortunately laughed too much at his maſter.

Lord Townly's ſervant was a little too baſhful—We are told he has a place at Court; ſo there are ſome hopes he will mend of that fault by the time he has been a little longer there.

So much for the Gentlemen; now for the Ladies.

Miſs Hodges made an incomparable Lady Townly:—It is but common juſtice to ſay, that this Lady performed her part in a ſtyle far ſuperior to any thing we have ever ſeen on the Theatres. The beauty of her face, the melody of her voice, the

C 3   elegance

elegance of her perfon; her eyes amazingly expreffive! her eafy yet graceful deportment, were fuch as have never been united in any female who was an actrefs by profeffion: One might juftly fay with Milton—" Grace was in all her fteps, Heaven in her " eye; in every gefture, dignity and fpirit!"

Mifs Harvey, in Lady Wronghead, was as natural as could be expected from a maiden Lady, who was to appear the mother of fuch well grown children; and the truly maternal affection fhe feemed to fhew them, makes one regret that fhe has none of her own:—If fhe perform that part again, we would recommend lefs motion of her body and eyes, and more of her arms.

Modefty, and the fober joys of domeftic life, could not be better expreffed than by Mifs Clarke, in Lady Grace. We will not fay fhe was without a fault; for fhe did not exprefs near enough of feeling for her friend Lady Townly.

The two Mifs Hopkins we have feen to more advantage in various characters; but, perhaps, they did not think it neceffary to exert themfelves in a country company.

Monfieur

Monfieur le Teffier might with great reafon be diffatisfied, if we were to conclude without paying him that compliment which is due to his merit in the after-piece of Pygmalion; we could enlarge upon it with pleafure, were not Mr. Garrick alive; but as he is, and we hope will long continue, we would not, by invidious comparifons, difpleafe one by whom we have been fo often pleafed; however, this much we muft fay, that for juft, natural, lively, expreffive, animated action, we never faw any rival or competitor to our Englifh Rofcius, at leaft none that ought to give him the fmalleft degree of jealoufy, but Monfieur le Teffier.

After the play, Lord Villiers entertained the company with a moft elegant and fumptuous fupper, and a ball. There was a profufion of the choiceft wines, and moft exquifite viands: and it was a very doubtful point with the company, which they fhould moft admire, his Lordfhip's elegant tafte, his engaging affability, or his unbounded hofpitality.

Every part of the entertainment was conducted with the greateft propriety; and the moft polite attention was paid to every perfon prefent.

VERSES

VERSES,

SAID TO HAVE BEEN WRITTEN BY LADY
B——T L——E, ON SEEING THE PADLOCK *
PERFORMED AT WESTON, THE SEAT OF SIR
HENRY BRIDGMAN, BART.

IN Albion's isle, ere hoary Time grew old,
The fairies wish'd a midnight feast to hold;
A council call'd of elves and fairy sprites,
The gliding revellers of star-light nights:
The subject strange requires a nice debate
To solve new doubts, and ev'ry caution state;
Where they should hold their gaily sportive rites,
Their fears all ca'm'd, the fairy queen invites;
To Weston's woods the bidden guests repair,
Enchanting seat! of all that's wisely fair.
The rural scene with wonder they revise,
Eclips'd by nought but fair Eliza's † eyes;
Her pleasing form, and gentle winning grace,
Breathe gay delight, serene, o'er ev'ry place;
Redundant smiles her dimpled cheeks display,
And steal e'en Envy's venom'd shafts away.

* Leonora, — Miss Pigott, ⎤ Daughters of Lord
Mungo, — Miss Pigott, ⎦ Pigott.
Leander, — Master Henry Bridgman.
Ursula, — Miss Bridgman
† L——y B————n.

Fairies

Fairies and jealous mortals jointly own,
The rose not half so fragrant, newly blown ;
That Hybla's sweets amidst her tresses play ;
She softer, milder, sweeter far than they.
The Fairy Queen reluctant feels her pow'r,
And steals to rest beneath a hawthorn flow'r :
First bids her train the fair Eliza tend,
Guard o'er her charms, and to them awful bend.
Pleas'd with the charge, the blooming loves advance,
They sing, they play, they weave the twining dance ;
They first relate Diego's ill starr'd fate,
In age lamenting for a youthful mate.
Next they rehearse the pangs of Henry's love,
In strains as smooth as Cytherea's dove ;
Thou lovely boy, no future pain shall own,
Love's pointed arrow shall by thee be thrown, }
And Leonora love but thee alone.

Aid me, ye Nine, with sprightly lines to grace
The well stole looks of Mungo's merry pace.
Nor let the careful Ursula bemoan,
My lays requite all merit save her own.
You prov'd that Nature yet could rival Art,
For sense and judgment grac'd your perfect part.
O beauteous maid, receive my humble pray'r ;
May Fate still mark you fortunate as fair :
May you in each new scene of busy life,
Play well the part of daughter, mother, wife ;

- Receive

Receive th' applause your merits juftly claim,
And yield to none in virtue or in fame.
In that firft page let Patfhull's fyren fhine,
Her air prevailing, and her voice divine;
Her dulcet lays and warbling notes proclaim
Her blithelt Philomel of Wefton's plain.
May Fairy pow'rs thefe pleafing ftrains requite,
Strew fragrant flow'rs, and tend your flocks by night;
Shed o'er your virgin hours content and reft,
And chace each aching forrow from your breaft.

    The mafque was ended and the bufy crew,
Eager of praife, to fair Eliza flew.
With grace benign, to each fhe juft decrees
That with the wifh they gain'd the pow'r to pleafe;
That each to Mab one acorn-cup fhould bear,
To prove their merit bore an equal fhare:
O'er the pale green they trip, and bounding ftray,
No fportive fawn fo innocent and gay;
To the arch'd bow'r their acorn goblets bear,
And wake their Queen, new conquefts to declare.
Jocund fhe fprings, with joy their tribute views,
Fills them with æther and ambrofial dews;
Then leads the feftive dance by Cynthia's light,
And by approving does their toils requite:
Quick o'er their eye-lids fheds their languid juice,
Diftill'd from cowflips for lov'd Oberon's ufe;
To balmy fleep they drop, by Mab infpir'd,
By all regretted, and by all admir'd.

PROLOGUE

PROLOGUE

TO ALL FOR LOVE, ACTED AT BLENHEIM-HOUSE,
IN THE SUMMER 1718. WRITTEN BY BISHOP
HOADLEY, AND SPOKEN BY LADY BATEMAN,
WHO ACTED CLEOPATRA.

WHILE ancient dames and heroes in us live,
And scenes of Love and War we here revive;
Greater in each, in each more fortunate,
Than all that ever ages past call'd great;
O Marlbro'! think not wrong that I thee name,
And first do homage to thy brighter fame.
Beauty and Virtue with each other strove
To move and recompence thy early love;
Beauty with Egypt's Queen could never boast,
And Virtue she ne'er knew, or quickly lost:
A soul so form'd and cloath'd Heav'n must design,
For such a soul, and such a form as thine.

But call'd from soft repose, and Beauty's charms,
Thy louder fame is spoke in feats of arms.
The fabled stories of great Philip's son,
By thy great deeds the world has seen outdone;
The Cæsars that Rome boasted yield their bays,
And own, in justice, thy superior praise:

C 6   They

They fought the empire of the world to gain,
But thou to break the haughty tyrant's chain ;
They fought t' enflave mankind, but thou to free
Whole nations from detefted flavery :
" Their guilty paths to grandeur taught to hate
" By Virtue, nor blufh for being great."

This heap of ftones which Blenheim's palace frame,
Rofe in this form, a monument to thy name ;
This heap of ftones muft crumble into fand,
But thy great name fhall thro' all ages ftand.
In Fate's dark book I fee thy long-liv'd name,
And thus the certain prophecy proclaim :
" One fhall arife who fhall thy deeds rehearfe,
" Not in arch'd roofs, or in fufpected verfe,
" But in plain annals of each glorious year,
" With pomp of Truth the ftory fhall appear:
" Long after Blenheim's walls fhall moulder'd lie,
" Or, blown by winds, to diftant countries fly,
" By him fhall thy great actions all furvive,
" And by thy name fhall his be taught to live."

Oh! cherifh the remains of life ; furvey
Thofe years of glory which can ne'er decay ;
Enjoy the beft reward below allow'd,
The mem'ry of paft actions great and good.

LINES,

L I N E S,

WRITTEN ON SEEING LADY EAST PERFORM THE
CHARACTER OF ALMERIA, IN THE MOURNING
BRIDE, AT SIR WILLIAM EAST'S THEATRE,
AT HULL-PLACE, IN BERKS.

IN polifh'd Eaft's fair frame behold
All that the Poets feign'd of old ;
Her form as elegant and true
As ever Grecian artift drew ;
Her treffes Nature's colour wear,
Which fhew her iv'ry neck more fair,
Mufic and energy unite
To make her accents breathe delight !
We feel her fympathetic pow'rs,
And all Almeria's woes are ours.

ON THE QUEEN'S PRESENTING MRS. THOMAS,
THE BISHOP OF WINCHESTER'S LADY, WITH
A HORSE AND CABRIOLE CHAIR, FOR HER
AIRINGS IN FARNHAM-PARK.

ANNO 1778.

THO' Snip the beft of Queens forfakes,
  To ftarve he's in no danger :
At Court may be the higheft racks,
  But here's as deep a manger.

Th

The Bishop, good and kind to all,
   Will keep him fat and thriving;
Already he has got a stall,
   And will have a good living.

INSCRIPTION FOR A BENCH BENEATH A FAVOU-RITE TREE.

AVAUNT! ye noisy sons of wine,
Nor round your brows *my* roses twine:
'Twas not for you that Flora here
Bestow'd those beauties of the year.

But ye, who social converse love,
Or ye whom softer passions move,
Come pass with me the careless day,
Or in my groves in freedom stray.

For *you* this verdant turf is spread,
For *you* this beach here rears its head,
For *you* has Flora scatter'd here
The varied beauties of the year.

IN THE CHURCH-YARD OF BROMLEY, IN KENT.

WRITTEN BY THE LATE JOHN HAWKESWORTH,
L. L. D.

Near this place lies the body of
E L I Z A B E T H   M O N K,
who departed this life on the 17th day of Aug. 1753,
aged 101.
She was the Widow of John Monk, late of this parish,
blacksmith,
her second husband,
to whom she had been a wife near fifty years.
By him she had no children ;
and of the issue of her first marriage none lived to the
second.————
But virtue
would not suffer her to be childless.
An infant, to whom, and to whose father and uncles,
she had been nurse,
(such is the uncertainty of temporal posterity !)
became dependent upon strangers for the necessaries of
life ;
to him she afforded the protection of a mother.
This parental charity was returned with filial affection;
and she was supported in the feebleness of age
by him whom she had cherished in the helplessness of
infancy.

LET

LET IT BE REMEMBERED,
That there is no ftation in which induftry will not
obtain power to be liberal,
nor any character on which liberality will not confer
Honour.
She had been long prepared,
by a fimple and unaffected piety,
for that awful moment which, however delayed, is
univerfally fure.
How few are allowed an equal time of probation!
How many by their lives appear to prefume upon more!
To preferve the memory of this perfon,
but yet more to perpetuate the leffon of her life,
this Stone was erected by voluntary contribution.

IN THE CATHEDRAL AT BRISTOL.

IN MEMORY OF MRS. MASON, WHO DIED AT THE
HOTWELLS, IN 1767.

TAKE, holy earth, all that my foul holds dear,
    Take that beft gift which Heav'n fo lately gave :
To Briftol's fount I bore, with trembling care,
    Her faded form : fhe bow'd to tafte the wave,

And,

And died. Does youth, does beauty, read the line ?
   Does fympathetic fear their breafts alarm ?
Speak, dead Maria ! breathe a ftrain divine :
   Ev'n from the grave thou fhalt have pow'r to charm:
Bid them be chafte, be innocent, like thee ;
   Bid them in duty's fphere as meekly move ;
And, if fo fair, from vanity as free,
   As firm in friendfhip, and as fond in Love :
Tell them, though 'tis an awful thing to die,
   ('Twas ev'n to thee) yet the dread path once trod,
Heav'n lifts its everlafting portals high,
   And bids " the pure in heart behold their God."

W. MASON.

EPITAPH

ON MISS DRUMMOND, DAUGHTER OF THE ARCH-
BISHOP OF YORK.

BY MR. MASON.

HERE fleeps--what once was beauty, once was grace,
   Grace, that with fenfe and tendernefs combin'd
To form that harmony of foul and face,
   Where Beauty fhines the mirror of the mind.

Such

Such was the maid, who, in the morn of youth,
 In virgin innocence, in Nature's pride,
Bleft with each art which owes its charm to Truth,
 Sunk in her father's fond embrace, and dy'd.

He weeps!—Oh venerate the holy tear!
 Faiths lends her aid to eafe Affliction's load;
The parent mourns his child upon her bier,
 The Chriftian yields an Angel to his God.

A FRAGMENT ON AN EPIC POEM.

BY MISS AIKIN.

SENT BY THAT LADY TO DR. PRIESTLEY, ON
THE MORNING SUCCEEDING THE EVENING'S
LOSS OF A GAME AT CHESS.

[Thefe are the Verfes which the Monthly Reviewers
 fo juftly regret were omitted in the publifhed Collection of Mifs Aikin's Poems.]

WHEN now the hoftile maid refus'd to yield,
The honours of the well difputed field;
When her firm phalanx, wedg'd in clofe array,
Prefs'd tow'rds the gaol, and turn'd the doubtful day.

The

The knight defpair'd by open force to gain
Victorious laurels on the chequer'd plain :
And long revolv'd, within his wily breaft,
What friendly pow'r would aid his conqueft beft.
Diftrefs'd by doubt, and urg'd by deep defpair,
At length to Morpheus he addrefs'd his pray'r ;
A gentle, harmlefs, inoffenfive pow'r,
And ne'er invok'd in fighting fields before.
He turn'd, obfervant to the fetting fun,
Thrice yawn'd, and his petition thus begun :

" O thou ! whófe equal, mild, and grateful fway,
" The wretched welcome, and the great obey,
" If e'er, with murmur'd fpells of magic found,
" I've fpread thy empire ev'n on holy ground,
" 'Till drowfy vapours crept from pew to pew,
" 'Till all the nodding audience bow'd to you,
" And hung their heads like flow'rs beneath the
    " dew ;
" In conftant flumbers feal thofe hoftile eyes,
" And let my troops th' unwary fce furprize.
" My grateful hand to thee fhall confecrate
" An ample folio, of ftupendous weight.
" Words of fuch opiate virtue fhall compofe
" The foporific, foft, lothean dofe ;
" No mortal eye-lids fhall refift the charm,
" No Dutchman's phlegm againft its influence arm.
" Thy

" Thy moſt rebellious ſubjects then ſhall know
" Thy pow'r, and to thy leaden ſceptre bow !"

He ſaid, when Morpheus from a cloud deſcends,
And o'er the female chief his wand extends ;
Then from her eye the martial ardour fled,
And ev'ry project vaniſh'd from her head.
She yawns, ſhe nods, no more o'erlooks the field,
In leaden, deep, and death-like ſlumbers ſeal'd.

Now, ſcatter'd wide, her broken ſquadrons fly,
Nobles and pawns in wild diſorder lie.
Ruin ſucceeds, ‘confuſion, ſhameful flight,
And her pale troops grew paler with affright ;
While ardent Hope the conqu'ring bands o'erſpread
With a new fluſh of more enliven'd red.
At length the Queen, the captiv'd Queen is loſt,
And inſtant fate o'erwhelms the ſcatter'd hoſt.

So when Ulyſſes, from the Trojan realm,
Ten weary nights had waken'd at the helm ;
Juſt as his native ſhore ſalutes his eyes,
And Ithaca's blue hills in proſpect riſe ;
By Sleep's reſiſtleſs charms the chief oppreſs'd,
Exhauſted, ſinks to momentary reſt,
Back o'er the bounding waves the veſſel flew,
And tempeſt toſs'd his ſhatter'd bark anew.

But

But Morpheus, ever prone to raife th' oppref's'd,
To foothe the fad, and fuccour the diftref's'd,
Around the vanquifh'd maid's inglorious head,
With lenient care, his downy pinions fpread ;
Plac'd her by rural groves and chryftal ftreams,
And footh'd her fancy with aufpicious dreams.
Cheer'd with frefh hopes, fhe veiws the morning light,
And burns with ardour to renew the fight.

THE PLEIADES.

WITH Devon's girl fo blithe and gay,
I well could like to fport and play :
With J—rfey would the time beguile,
And laugh and titter, fneer and fmile :
With B—v—rie I fhould like to fin,
With D———— I could only grin ;
With C—l—fle wifdom's plan purfue,
With—M———— I would nothing do ;
To this vain town I'd bid adieu,
To pafs my life, and think with Crewe!

THE PLANETS--A COMPANION TO THE PLEIADES.

WITH charming Cholmondeley well one might
Pass all the day and half the night;
From Montagu's more fertile mind,
Perpetual source of pleasure find;
Of Tully's Latin, Homer's Greek,
With learn'd Carter I could speak:
While to politeness, wit and sense,
Greville can teach indifference:
With grave Macauley I'd debate
The means to save a sinking state:
With Thrale converse in purest ease
Of letters, life, and languages;
But if I dare to talk with Crewe,
My heart, my peace, my ease—adieu

LADY CRAVEN, ON DREAMING SHE SAW HER HEART AT HER FEET.

SAID TO BE WRITTEN BY HERSELF. *

WHEN Nature, tir'd with thought, was sunk to rest,
And all my senses were by sleep possess'd,

* It has been likewise ascribed to Madame de Vauclufe, gouvernante to her Ladyfhip's children.

Sweet

Sweet fleep! that balmy comfort brings
Alike to beggars and defpotic kings ;
I dreamt of peace I never felt before,
I dreamt my heart was lying on the floor.
I view'd it, ftrange to tell! with joyful eyes,
And, ftranger ftill, without the leaft furprife !
Elated with the fight, I fmiling fat,
Exulting o'er the victim at my feet ;
But foon with words of anguifh thus addrefs'd
This painful, fweet difturber of my breaft :
" Say, bufy, lively, trembling, hopping thing,
" What new difafter haft thou now to bring,
" To torture with thy fears my tender frame,
" Who muft for all her ills thee only blame ?
" Speak now, and tell me why, ungrateful gueft,
" For ten years paft thou haft denied me reft ?
" That in my bofom thou waft nurs'd, 'tis true,
" And with my life and with my ftature grew.
" At firft fo fmall were all thy wants, that I
" Vainly imagin'd I could ne'er deny
" Whate'er thy fancy afk'd.—Alas! but now
" I find thy wants my ev'ry fenfe outgrow :
" And ever having, ever wanting more,
" A pow'r to pleafe, to give, or to adore.
" Say, why like other hearts doft thou not bear
" With callous apathy each worldly care ?
" Why doft thou fhriek at Envy's horrid cries ?
" In thee Compaffion Hatred's place fupplies.

" Why

" Why not with malice treat malicious men ?
" Why ever pity where thou fhould'ft condemn ?
" Why, at the hearing of a difmal tale,
" Doft thou with forrow turn my vifage pale ?
" Why, when diftrefs in any fhape appears,
" Doft thou diffolve my very foul in tears ?
" Why in thy fecret folds is Friendfhip bred ?
" In other hearts its very name is dead.
" Why, if keen wit and learned fenfe draw nigh,
" Doft thou with emulation beat fo high ?
" And while approving wifh to be approv'd,
" And when you love wifh more to be belov'd ?
" Why not, in cold indiff'rence ever clad,
" Alike unmov'd regard the good and bad ?
" Why doft thou wafte my youthful bloom with care,
" And facrifice myfelf, that I may fhare
" Diftrefs in others? Why wilt thou adorn
" Their days with rofes, and leave me a thorn ?"

But here I faw it heave an heavy figh,
And thus in fweeteft founds it did reply:

" Ah! ceafe, Eliza! ceafe thy fpeech unjuft,
" Thine heart has e'er fulfill'd its facred truft,
" And ever will its tender manfion ferve,
" Nor can it this reproach from thee deferve;
" Againft my dictates murm'ring have I found,
" Which thus has laid me bleeding on the ground.

" Compare

" Compare thyself in this same hour depriv'd
" Of this soft heart, from whence are all deriv'd
" The same bewitching graces which adorn,
" And make thy face appear like beauteous morn:
" With me its brilliant ornaments are fled,
" And all thy features, like thy soul, are dead.
" 'Tis I that make thee other's pleasure share,
" And in a sister's joy forget thy care;
" 'Tis by my dictates thou art taught to find
" A godlike pleasure in a godlike mind ;
" That makes thee oft relieve a stranger's woes,
" And often fix those friends that would be foes.
" 'Tis I that tremblingly have taught thine ear
" To cherish music; and 'tis I appear
" In all its softest dress, when to the hearts
" Of all beholders my dear voice imparts
" Harmonic strains : 'tis not because 'tis fine,
" For ev'ry note that's felt is surely mine.
" In smoothest numbers all that I indite,
" For 'tis I taught thy fearful hand to write ;
" My genius has with watchful care supplied
" What Education to thy sex denied ;
" Made Sentiment and Nature all combine
" To melt the reader in each flowing line,
" 'Till they in words this feeling truth impart,
" She needs no more who will consult the heart ;
" And own, in reading what is writ by thee,
" No study ever could improve like me.

Vol. VI.   D   And

" And when thy bloom is gone, thy beauty flows,
" And laughing Youth to wrinkled Age is grown,
" Thy actions, writings, friendship, which I gave,
" Still shall remain, an age beyond the grave,
" Then do not thus displac'd let me remain,
" But take me to thy tender breast again."

" Yes, soft persuader, (I return'd) I will;
" And if I am deceiv'd, deceive me still."

Seduc'd I was in haste; then stooping low,
Soon reinstated my sweet, pleasing foe;
And, waking, found it had nor less nor more
Than all the joys, the pangs it had before.

ADDRESS TO LADY CRAVEN's HEART.

No wonder, little fluttering thing,
That you so soon should leap and spring
To Craven's fair and beauteous breast,
Where gods themselves would wish to rest!
But tell me, trifler, tell me, why
You could from such a mansion fly,
Where ev'ry virtue you'd in store?
Miser—what could you wish for more?
Say, did you long at will to roam,
And quite forsake your native home?

Or

Or had you been too clofe confin'd,
And for fweet Liberty you pin'd?
Oh! had I found you in fome grove,
Cafket of Friendfhip and of Love!
I'd place thee, wand'ring heart!—by mine;
Uniting both with Friendfhip's twine:
Of fuch a jewel—fafe poffeft,
Not worlds fhould tear thee from my breaft;
Exulting round the rural plains,
Boaft of the prize—to nymphs and fwains.
But hufh!—my ruftic mufe!—nor dare
To wifh a friend fo great, fo fair;
For vain will all thofe wifhes prove,
Then hide thee in thy lonely grove!
But if fair Craven e'er fhou'd ftray,
By my lone cottage bend her way,
I'd lead her to my fhady feat,
And lay my heart, too—at her feet!
Which, if fhe'd condefcend to view,
She'd find it conftant, firm, and true;
To welcome her with many' a bound,
'Twould leap with joy—and dance around!

OLIVIA, THE HUMBLE COTTAGER.

 TO

TO LADY CRAVEN'S HEART, LYING ON THE FLOOR.

RETURN! thy native bosom grace,
　　Where charms unnumber'd play;
Fit rival to its kindred face,
　　So beautifully gay.

Once more, Oh! let the trio meet,
　　Never again to part;
Of all thy sex, who boasts so sweet
　　A bosom, face, or heart.

FRANZEL.

Near Reading, Aug. 17, 1780.

THE RIGHT HONOURABLE AUTHORESS.

ON the top of the flow'r-deck'd poetical mount,
A tenth Muse, I dare, *sans* offending, to count,
　　Apollo who no way disgraces;
In her wit her nine sisters by far she excells,
For charms she out-rivals the first of our belles,
　　United in her all the Graces.
" I know her full well, cries the Cyprian Queen,
" 'Tis CRAVEN, my fav'rite beauty, you mean.

* Parnassus.

EPILOGUE, *

EPILOGUE, *

SPOKEN BY MRS. WOFFINGTON, AT THE OPEN-
ING OF THE THEATRE IN DRURY-LANE,
1747.

BY DR. SAMUEL JOHNSON.

SWEET doings, truly! we are finely fobb'd!
And at one ftroke of all our pleafures robb'd!
No beaux behind the fcenes!—'tis innovation!
Under the fpecious name of reformation!
Public Complaint, forfooth, is made a puff,
Senfe, order, decency, and fuch like ftuff.
But arguments like thefe are mere pretence,
The Beaux, 'tis known, ne'er give the leaft offence,
Are men of chafteft conduct, and amazing fenfe!
Each actrefs now a lock'd-up nun muft be,
And prieftly managers muft keep the key.
I know their felfifh reafons; tho' they tell us,
While fmarts, and wits, and other pretty fellows,
Murmur their paffions to our flutt'ring hearts,
The ftage ftands ftill, and we neglect our parts.
But how miftaken in this filly notion!
We hear 'em talk without the leaft emotion.

* See the Prologue in Dodfley's Collection, Vol. I.

Juft,

Juſt, as our tea, we ſip each tender ſtrain,
Too weak to warm the heart, or reach the brain.
If harmleſs, why are we debarr'd our rights?
Damſels diſtreſs'd have ever found their knights.
Shall we, the Dulcineas of the ſtage,
In vain aſk ſuccour in this fighting age?
Will you, choice ſpirits, who direct the town,
Suffer ſuch impoſitions to go down?
Can it be thought this law will ever paſs,
While doors are only wood, and windows glaſs?
Beſides, our play-houſe guards are paſſive men:
Strike without fear; they muſt not ſtrike again.
Ev'n Fribble here, to draw his ſword may venture,
May curſe the Creters, beat his man, and enter——
The jealous Moor not roars in louder ſtrains,
Than all our nymphs for loſs of abſent ſwains——
" We had been happy, tho' the houſe had fail'd,
" Maſters and all, had not this ſcheme prevail'd.
" For ever now farewel the plumed beaux,
" Who make ambition to conſiſt in cloaths.
" Farewel coquetry, and all green-room joys,
" Ear-thrilling whiſpers, Deard's deluding toys,
" Soul-melting flatt'ry, which ev'n prudes can move,
" Sighs—tears—and all the circumſtance of love,
" Farewel!———————
" But oh! ye dreadful critics, whoſe rude throats
" Can make both play'rs and maſters change their
    notes,
                        " 'Tis

" 'Tis in your pow'r—you any lengths will run,
" Help us; or else—our occupation's gone."

V E R S E S

AT THE REQUEST OF A GENTLEMAN TO WHOM
A LADY HAD GIVEN A SPRIG OF MYRTLE.

BY THE SAME.

WHAT hopes, what terrors does thy gift create,
Ambiguous emblem of uncertain Fate!
The myrtle (ensign of supreme command,
Consign'd by Venus to Melissa's hand)
Not less capricious than a reigning fair,
Oft favours, oft rejects a lover's pray'r:
In myrtle shades oft sings the happy swain,
In myrtle shades despairing ghosts complain;
The myrtle crowns the happy lovers heads,
Th' unhappy lovers graves the myrtle spreads;
Oh! then the meaning of thy gift impart,
And ease the throbbings of an anxious heart;
Soon must this bough, as you shall fix his doom,
Adorn Philander's head, or grace his tomb.

VERSES

VERSES

ON THE APPROACH OF WINTER.

BY THE SAME.

AUTUMNAL leaves apace do fade,
And Winter ſhows its hoary head,
    With clouds and winds auſtere:
Th' enamell'd flow'r in earth is laid,
And lies conceal'd in Nature's bed,
    'Till Sol revolves the year.

The feather'd throng prepare for flight,
The woods no ſhelter yield at night;
    Unrob'd their bow'rs appear:
The ſportſman views, with true delight,
The new-reap'd fields expoſe to fight
    The haunts of tim'rous hare.

To town, my Lord, with eager haſte
Repairs, and makes his dwelling-place
    At Arthur's or at White's:
Nor time her Ladyſhip doth waſte,
But ſeeks the route ſhe oft hath grac'd,
    And ſhone at whiſt whole nights.

The

The ſtreets ſhall now with flambeaux blaze ;
The gay reſort to balls and plays,
    And Winter's joys poſſeſs ;
While ſons of mirth in roundelays,
At feſtive board their voices raiſe,
    And Bacchus' pow'r confeſs.

The ſoldier now, from direful War,
Retires with honourable ſcar,
    With Cælia to engage :
While ſhe, more bright than morning ſtar,
Poſſeſs'd with ev'ry grace and air,
    Unequal War doth wage.

The Pluraliſt, with ſimp'ring cheek,
And ſtall-fed ſkin ſo ſmooth and ſleek,
    His tything circuit ends :
Tho' tythes he once a year doth ſeek,
His Curate preaches once a week,
    But oft with poor amends :

The Rector touches all the pelf,
And Curate ſtarves t'enrich himſelf,
    God's word is Mammon made :
While he, a lazy pamper'd elf,
Scarce pulls a book from off the ſhelf :
    His function is a trade.

         The

The Doctor, juft at death arriv'd,
Fearing of fee to be depriv'd,
    Ere ended is the farce;
To finifh recipe he ftriv'd,
That done, or live or die he's brib'd,
    Affur'd it is his laft.

E L E G Y

ON THE DEATH OF DR. ROBERT LEVET.

BY THE SAME.

CONDEMN'D to Hope's delufive mine,
As on we toil from day to day,
By fudden blafts, or flow decline,
Our focial comforts drop away.

Well tried thro' many a varying year,
See Levet to the grave defcend;
Officious, innocent, fincere,
Of ev'ry friendlefs name the friend.

Yet ftill he fills Affection's eye,
Obfcurely wife, and coarfely kind;
Nor, letter'd Arrogance, deny
Thy praife to merit unrefin'd.

When

When fainting Nature call'd for aid,
And hov'ring Death prepar'd the blow.
His vig'rous remedy difplay'd
The pow'r of Art without the fhow.

In Mis'ry's darkeft caverns known,
His ufeful care was ever nigh;
Where hopelefs Anguifh pour'd his groan,
And lonely Want retir'd to die.

No fummons mock'd by chill delay,
No petty gain difdain'd by pride;
The modeft wants of ev'ry day,
The toil of ev'ry day fupplied.

His virtues walk'd their narrow round,
Nor made a paufe, nor left a void;
And fure th' Eternal Mafter found
His fingle talent well employ'd.

The bufy day, the peaceful night,
Unfelt, uncounted, glided by;
His frame was firm, his powers were bright,
Tho' now his eightieth year was nigh.

Then with no throbbing fiery pain,
No cold gradations of decay,
Death broke at once the vital chain,
And forc'd his foul the neareft way.

ON A PINCUSHION.

OF all the trinkets that the toilet grace,
The Pincuſhion deſerves the higheſt place.
When balls or operas invite the fair,
How could ſhe ſet her knots, or curl her hair,
Did not th' important pin each air ſupply,
Subduing ſtubborn plaits that ſtand awry ?
The little pin ſtill finds an uſeful place
In mobs, in lappets, and in Bruſſels lace :
The modeſt Pilgrim o'er the ſhoulders draws,
Or from the well-plac'd peeper gains applauſe ;
In every office it performs is bleſt,
Now to her eye is neareſt, now her breaſt.

Others may to the milliner repair,
But Sylvia deigns not to be furniſh'd there :
Cupid himſelf ſupplies her magazines,
And works his pointed arrows into pins :
No wonder ev'ry look ſhou'd wound a heart,
Each Corkin that adorns her is a dart.

ON AURELIA SLEEPING.

WRITTEN BY A YOUTH AT THE AGE OF FIFTEEN.

I.

SEE! where the bright Aurelia lies
  In yonder vi'let fmelling bow'r;
Sleep, gentle Sleep, has clos'd her eyes,
  Ye Cupids! guard the happy hour.

II.

Zephyrs! play foft around her breaft;
  Fan from her lips the fipping fly,
That dares fuch beauty to moleft,
  At whofe command I live or die.

III.

Silence! ye feather'd, warb'ling throng!
  Awhile your harmony forbear;
Awhile fufpend each rural fong,
  Left you awake my fleeping fair.

IV. So

IV.

So may you never, never hear
   The gun dread-founding thro' the air,
So may you never, never fear
   The cruel school-boy's limy snare.

THE GIRDLE OF VENUS.

A FABLE FROM THE GREEK.

FOR GROWN LADIES.

WHEN Jupiter's high mettl'd dame
   (As we read in Dan Homer the story)
Had a mind his cold breast to inflame,
   And to shine with additional glory.

She order'd her peacocks and car,
   And then flew to the Queen of the doves,
Who liv'd from her palace not far,
   In the midst of the Graces and Loves.

" Dear Venus," thus flow'd her smooth speech,
   " Prythee lend me your cestus to-day,
" To repair a small conjugal breach ;
   " And be quick, for I soon must away—

                        " I must

" I muſt haſte to unite a good pair,
  " Who took care of me when I was young,
" And each other now hardly can bear,
  " Having both been by Jealouſy ſtung."

Her ſecret deſign ſhe conceal'd,
  (So ſhould women act when they're married)
For ſhe knew if it once was reveal'd,
  It would ſoon round Olympus be carried.—

The blithe Goddeſs not gueſſing her drift,
  On her waſte tied the ceſtus of pleaſure,
And the cloud-ruler's ſiſter, then ſwift
  As his eagle, whirl'd off with her treaſure.

In this girdle was curiouſly ſtitch'd
  The attractions which toying inſpire,
And moreover, 'twas finely enrich'd
  With all arts to re-kindle deſire.

In this girdle, good-humour and eaſe,
  Sweet words and fond looks were expreſs'd,
A perpetual endeavour to pleaſe,
  And a face with gay ſmiles ever dreſs'd.

Poſſeſs'd of ſo rich a machine,
  She was eager its virtues to try,
And then leaving the love-darting Queen,
  Shot a thouſand bright beams from each eye.

To the Thund'rer fhe then, as by chance,
 Half her beauties with cunning difplay'd,
From her eye fhot a languifhing glance,
 And then glided away like a fhade.

But fhe dazzl'd the eyes of grim Jove,
 Who embrac'd her with conjugal arms,
And within a delicious alcove,
 He enjoy'd with new fpirit her charms.

Ye wives, lend an ear to this fample
 Of the Grecian bard's fhrewdnefs and art,
And by politic Juno's example,
 Learn to conquer a hufband's cold heart.

When the paffion of Love's in its wane,
 And ye ceafe to be objects of joy,
Ye muft try the cold heart to regain,
 By thofe beauties which never will cloy.

THE PIGEON's CHOICE.

To ev'ry fair a pigeon rov'd,
By ev'ry fair alike belov'd :
Where'er he flew, the female train
Practife their wiles his heart to gain ;

Bridle

Bridle the neck, and bill and coo,
And imitate what women do.
At length he found that too much joy,
Muſt ſoon his vig'rous health deſtroy;
So thought it prudent to give over,
Aſſume the huſband, drop the lover.

At firſt, the Fan-tail nymph he tries,
Who, in a moment, met his eyes :
Her heart exults with inward pride,
And Fancy fix'd her for his bride.
Secure of conqueſt, ſhe neglected
The real charms the youth expected.
No gentle manners, no conceſſion ;
All muſt be left to her diſcretion :
Whilſt vanity and affectation
Supplied the place of ſenſe and ſtation.
" He could not anſwer to his conſcience,
" To be confin'd to pride and nonſenſe :
" A miſtreſs thus was right and civil,
" But, in a wife, they were the devil !"
So left the nymph to ſtrut alone,
Regardleſs of her idle moan.

The Carrier, a pigeon ſleek,
With ruddy bill, and ſnowy neck,
Caught his deſires ; but yet the dame
Had but a ſort of doubtful fame.

He faw fhe rambled round the county,
And guefs'd fhe might difperfe her bounty.
He knew fhe feldom kept the houfe,
And needs muft make a wretched fpoufe.
Never at eafe but on the wing!
So dropt the airy giddy thing.

The Cropper next, a ftately fair!
Claim'd his affection and his care;
But, to his forrow, foon he found
Her principles and mind unfound.
She boafted much her great defcent,
" She was not for the vulgar meant:
" Yet fhe would yield to his requeft,
" Provided he would make her neft.
" Her noble limbs were quite unfit
" To do the drudg'ry of a cit."
He rais'd his head, his anger grew,
Flapping his wings, away he flew.

An hundred other forts he tried,
Some promis'd fair, fome half denied;
But what rais'd moft his indignation,
Was Pride deep fix'd by Education.

Clofe in a farmer's yard he faw
The Common Pigeon, deep in ftraw:

He

He view'd her modeſt humble mien,
Her beauteous feathers neat and clean :
He ſaw her earning hard her food,
And thought ſhe'd bring a healthy brood.
His judgment fix'd her in his mind,
He lov'd and courted,—ſhe prov'd kind.
Of her poſſeſs'd, he found how vain
Were all the trifling, giggling train.
No gadder ſhe, no affeɛtation !
No airs to give his mind vexation ;
Her thoughts were wholly on him bent,
Studious in all to give content.
With pleaſure on his bill ſhe hung,
Then hatch'd her eggs, or fed her young :
With her he found the charms that give
The bliſs, that makes it bliſs to live.

TO THE RIGHT HONOURABLE LORD VISCOUNT
PULTENEY.

WRITTEN IN THE YEAR 1747, AT WESTMINSTER-
SCHOOL.

BY GEORGE COLMAN.

TO you, my Lord, theſe lines I write,
Leſt you forget poor Coley quite,

(Who

(Who still is drudging in the College,
In slow pursuit of further knowledge :
With many a cruel lash his —— on,
To make him some time hence a parson ;
A judge, perhaps, or a physician,
Strolling on Ratcliffe's exhibition.)

While you with foreign monarchs dine,
Or sup with princes cross the Rhine ;
Idle your hours in lazy state,
Just as forgetful as you're great ;
Ramble to ev'ry court your rounds,
Draw when you please an hundred pounds ;
Despise expence, and dress out tawdry,
In cloaths of lace, and gay embroid'ry ;
Shine at the ball, and briskly dance,
As tho' you had been bred in France.
I hear too that your constant trade is
To ogle and ensnare the ladies,
Whose hearts, unwary, fire like tinder,
And waste away by love t'a cinder,
Whilst you are glad to see your pride
On all occasions gratified,
And disregard your friends at London,
Not caring tho' they're hang'd or undone.
" But hold (you cry) why this abuse ?
Pray hearken, Sir, to my excuse ;

Nor

Nor hurry with impetuous thought,
To blame your friend, ere he's in fault.
At th' Hague we had not time to reſt us,
Diſturbances did ſo moleſt us;
For you muſt know, theſe ſcoundrel Dutch
Rebel, for being *tax'd* too much.
Loyal and paſſive we obey on,
And bear all taxes they can lay on.
The Britiſh Lion now is couchant,
Grumbling, perhaps, but won't make much on't;
Taking with patient reſignation,
Whate'er's impos'd upon the nation.
In camp too, I'd but little leiſure,
My time was ſo fill'd up with pleaſure.
With all old ſchool-fellows ſo dear,
And Albemarle and Ligonier,
That I had ſcarce an hour to ſpare.
The Duke too ſhew'd me a review,
All that, at that time, he could do;
For you muſt know, at preſent writing,
Our armies have all done with fighting.
From hence to Hanover we went,
Liv'd in a round of merriment.
I had no time to ſcribble letters,
To you, dear Coley, or your betters."

My Lord, you're right, and we from hence
Will quite o'erlook your negligence.

But,

But, *sans* offence, may I enquire,
In what the prefent hours expire?
What pleafure or what ftudy beft
Your temper fuits, may I requeft?
I hear in law you're a proficient;
And other learning have fufficient;
Can folve a problem mathematic,
And read with eafe a Greek dramatic;
You're fkill'd in hiftory enough;
Of algebra have *quantum fuff.*
And are, by learned mens' tuition,
The quinteffence of erudition;
So vers'd in all that can be nam'd,
Ifis and Cam are quite afham'd,
And all their fcholars are downright fick,
To fee themfelves outdone at Leipfick.
Tho' I have long with ftudy mental
Labour'd at language Oriental,
Yet, in my foil, the Hebrew root
Has fcarcely made one fingle fhoot.

   I've now broke up, but have a tafk tho'
Harder than your's with Mr. Mafcow;
For mine's as knotty as the devil,
Your law and mafter both are civil;
With milder means to learning lead,
By diff'rent roads, with diff'rent fpeed,
Douglas and you keep gently jogging,
But I muft run the race with flogging.

                     ASHTED

ASHTED COT.*

TIR'D with the noife and fmoke of town,
  Its crowded ftreets and fumptuous fare,
To Afhted Cot we oft fteal down :
  Who wifh for Peace may find her there.

There ftretch the ample profpects wide,
  Fields, woods, down, hills and fpires appear ;
The tempting walk, the grateful ride,
  Invite thro' all the varied year.

Or there, or no where can be found,
  Health, ever rofy, ever gay ;
Content there tills his narrow ground,
  And fings the toils of life away.

No foreign dainties glitter there ;
  Yet rural plenty there is known ;
The home-rear'd poultry's oft your fare,
  And mutton fed on Banfted Down.

The garden, hemm'd in little fpace,
  Is glad its herbs and fruits to fend :
Ne'er is forgot the thankful grace,
  Nor wine to toaft the abfent friend.

* A villa belonging to T— T———, Efq. Afhted is a fmall
village between Epfom and Leatherhead, in Surry.

Nor

Nor Party's voice, nor Faction's roar,
  Their baleful influence there have shed;
Ill-nature never op'd the door,
  Nor Spleen once dar'd to shew her head.

Yet books their moral store display,
  And social wit and chat go round;
The muse there tunes her rustic lay,
  And Leisure loves th' enchanted ground.

Tho' Pride on humble scenes looks down,
  And longs in pomp to pass the hours,
There are, who gladly quit the town,
  For tranquil joys in Ashted bow'rs.

THE DYING RAKE's SOLILOQUY.

BY DR. BARTHOLOMEW.

IN the fever of Youth ev'ry pulse in a flame,
Regardless of Fortune, of Health, and of Fame,
Gay Pleasure my aim, and Profusion my pride,
No vice was untasted, no wish was denied.
Grown headstrong and haughty, capricious and vain,
Not decency aw'd me, nor laws could refrain;

The

The vigils of Comus and Venus I kept,
Tho' tired, not fated, in funfhine I flept:
All my appetites pall'd, I no pleafure enjoy'd,
Excefs made 'em taftelefs, their frequency cloy'd.
When my health and my fortune to riot gave way,
And my parts and my vigour felt total decay,
The Doctors were fent for, who, greedy of fees,
Engag'd that their fkill fhould remove the difeafe:
With looks moft important each fymptom was weigh'd,
And the farce of prefcription full gravely was play'd.

Reduc'd by their arts, and quite worn to a lath,
My carcafe was fent to the vultures at Bath.
When drench'd and well drain'd by the faculty there,
All the hope that remain'd was to try native air.
Scarce a doit in my purfe, or a drop in my veins,
To my old mortgag'd houfe they convey'd my remains;
No friend to affift me, no relation to grieve,
And fcarcely a bed my poor bones to receive;
With folitude curs'd, and tormented with pain,
Diftemper'd my body, diftracted my brain.

Thus from folly to vice, and from vice to the grave,
I fink, of my paffions the victim and flave.
No longer debauch, or companions deceive,
But, alarm'd at the vengeance I'd fain difbelieve,
With horrors foreboding defponding I lie,
Tho' tired of living, yet dreading to die.

The following is an Allegory on the Game of Quadrille. It was written by Mr. Congreve. See Swift's Letters, vol. ii. page 198.

SUBSTANCE OF AN INFORMATION TAKEN BEFORE ONE OF HIS MAJESTY'S JUSTICES OF THE PEACE.

THAT four Ladies of Quality, whom the deponent does not care to name, repair mightily to a certain convenient house, to meet four gallants, of the highest rank, whom the deponent would not name, but so far described, that two of them were of a swarthy, and two of a ruddy complexion (but he believes they were abominably painted) ; the gallants are called by these Ladies, by the fond names of Hercules, Cupid, Pitts, and the Gardener.

After a plentiful service of the most costly fish, they begin to play their tricks like the tumblers in Bartholomew Fair, upon a carpet ; strip is the word, and it has been known, that they have lately stripp'd a Gentleman who lately came into the house.

At first they begin very civilly, as, Madam, by your leave, or so, which the Lady is so good as seldom to refuse.

By

By a certain eſtabliſhed rule of precedency, every Lady has, in her turn, the choice of her gallant, and ſome have been known ſo unreaſonable, that after they have had three, they have called for a fourth.

Afterwards, it is ſhameful to relate the tricks that are played by the lewd pack ; ſometimes they are thrown on their backs, ſometimes on their bellies, and thus they make beaſts of one another; now hickledy-pickledy, and by and by you may ſee them a-top of one another.

Their diſcourſe is of a piece with their practiſe—The deponent has often heard them talk of their A—with as much eaſe as they do of their hands.—I have a black one, ſays one, and names the thing directly.—Mine is better than yours, ſays another, and names it.—Muſt I be laughed at, only becauſe I have a red one, ſays the third.

It is a conſtant rule, that if a Lady is called upon, ſhe muſt ſhow all.

What is monſtrous ; it has been known, that after a Lady has had ſix—ſhe has aſked a Gentleman if he could no more—and it has been known, that when the Ladies have been tired with their gallants, they

have

have called for fresh ones.—In short, those Ladies
have spent not only their pin-money, but their huf-
bands' estates, upon Hercules, Cupid, Pitts, and the
Gardener; and when they want ready money, they
commonly pawn their most valuable jewels.

S   O   N   G *.

SAYS Phœbe, why is gentle Love
A stranger to that mind,
Which pity and esteem can move,
Which can be just and kind?
Is it because you fear to prove
The ills that Love molest;
The jealous cares, the sighs that move
The captivated breast?
Alas! by some degree of woe,
We ev'ry bliss must gain;
That heart that ne'er a transport know,
That never felt a pain.

* First published in one of the daily Papers, in August, 1769,
as a production of Mr. Pope.

VERSES

V E R S E S

ON THE NEW BUILDINGS ERECTING BETWEEN BLOOMSBURY AND ST. GILES'S.

IN a doublet of ſtone, from the top of a ſteeple,
As *Brunſwick* look'd down on *the dregs of the people,*
The handſome new buildings the folks were erecting,
His vanity tickl'd, and ſet him reflecting,
That ſoon he ſhould ſee, by his Grace's aſſiſtance,
The *ſcum of the earth* ladled off to a diſtance.
The breed of St. Giles's, plump, tatter'd, and pert,
Underſtanding his muſings, replied, from the dirt :

" Winds blaſt your hard phiz, for a weathercock
   wizzard,
What is't that you grumble at thus in your gizzard ?
Tho' we are ſo low, and you mounted ſo high,
Your horns, you old cuckold, don't reach to the ſky :
Then look not, your haughtineſs, downward ſo glum ;
We can't be at once both the *dregs* and the *ſcum.*
What tho' my Lord Duke, your as hard-hearted
   neighbour,
Would ſtarve us with nine-pence a-day for our labour,
Or drive us afield like black cattle, a grazing,
He neither can pound us, nor wall the highways in.

Let

Let his bricklayers and mafons then build till they
     burſt,
And his ſtreets, and his houſes, and chapels be curſt ;
While pence will, for prog, purchaſe pudding or pye,
As here we've been bred, here we'll live till we die.
Your highneſs may vapour, with arms ſet a-kimbo,
And your Grace move the Houſe to commit us to
     limbo ;
We tremble as little at you as at him,
At a peace broken peer as *a beer* brewer's whim. *
Had ſots been but ſober, your worſhip had ne'er
Een raiſed thus aloft, cock-a-hoop in the air ;
To mug-houſe and mobs your high ſtation thus owing,
Keep o'er your own dunghill no longer thus crowing.
Should a ſtorm ever blow that ſhould topple you down,
Who, think you, would plaiſter the crack in your
     crown ?
Your friends, the True Blue, ſcour'd and turn'd at
     the dyer's,
Old Whigs grow new Tories, low churchmen high-
     flyers,
By Dukes, Lords and Knights, you'll be left in the
     lurch,
As ſure as you tumble from Bloomſbury-church.
The State in a ferment, poor Pelham departed,
Your Grandſon, God bleſs him, much too tender-
     hearted ;

  * This ſtatue was erected at the expence of his Majeſty's brewer.

In Faction's fierce flame Party still throwing oil,
'Till her long-simm'ring pot is just ready to boil,
Should her broth, over-heated, rise up to a brimmer,
And the Devil, to cool it, be sent with a skimmer,
The froth and the bubbles of Fortune and Birth,
From the top he'd take off, as *the scum of the earth* ;
While we, as he laughs in his sleeve to have got 'em,
The *dregs of the people,* sink safe to the bottom."

* * * *

ON SEEING CAPTAIN A——, AT MRS. CORNELY'S, DREST FANTASTICALLY.

'TIS said, that our soldiers so lazy are grown,
   With luxury, plenty, and ease,
That they more for their *carriage* than *courage* are
      known,
   And scarce know the use of a *piece* ;
Let them say what they will, since it nobody galls,
   And exclaim out still louder and louder ;
But there ne'er was more money expended in *balls,*
   Or a greater consumption of *powder.*

THE NORFOLKE TURNIPPE.

AN AUNCIENT TALE.

SOME countyes vaunte themfelves in pyes,
And fome in meate excelle ;
For Turnippes of enormous fize,
Faire Norfolke beares the belle.

Thilke tale an olde nurfe told to me,
Which I relate to you ;
And well I weene what nurfes fay,
Is facred all and true.

At midnighte houre a hardie knighte
Was pricking * o'er the ley, †
The ftarres and moone had lofte their lighte,
And he had lofte his waye.

The winde full loude and fharpe did blowe,
The clouds amaine did poure,
And fuch a night, as floryes fhewe,
Was nivir feene before.

* Riding.   † Meadow-ground.

I vaine

I vaine hee faughte full halfe the nighte,
Ne fhelter coulde hee fpie :
Pitie it were fo bolde a knighte
Y-fterv'd with cold fholde dye.

Now voices ftraunge affaile his eare,
And yet ne houfe was nie :
Thoughte hee, the Devil himfelf is here,
Preferve me God on hie !

Then fummon'd hee his courage hie,
And thus aloud 'gan call;
Fays, gyauntes, demons, come not nie,
For I defy you all !

When from a hollow turnippe neare
Out jump'd a living wighte ;
With friendly voice, and accent cleare,
He thus addrefs'd the knighte :—

Sir knighte, no demon dwelleth here,
Ne gyaunte keepes his houfe ;
But tway poor drovers, goodman Vere,
And honeft Robin Roufe.

We tweyne have taken fhelter here,
With oxen ninety-two ;
And if you'll enter nivir feare,
There's room enough for you.

E 5

ON THE OAK IN PENSHURST-PARK,

PLANTED ON THE BIRTH-DAY OF SIR PHILIP SIDNEY.

As I paſſed ſome weeks the laſt ſummer in the neighbourhood of Penſhurſt-park, in Kent, the ancient ſeat of the noble family of Sidney, I frequently had the pleaſure of riding among thoſe fine old woods. Mentioning this one day among ſome of my friends, a gentleman in company told us, that ſome years ſince, in a fall of timber that was made there for the uſe of the navy, a noble Oak, planted on the birth-day of the great Sir Philip Sidney, was, by miſtake, unhappily felled. We all agreed, that a tree, ſacred to the memory of ſo great a man, ought to have been preſerved inviolate from the edge of the axe.

Waller, in one of his poems, written at Penſhurſt, has the following lines on this Oak:

" Go, boy, and carve this paſſion on the bark
" Of yonder tree, which ſtands the ſacred mark
" Of noble Sidney's birth, when ſuch benign,
" Such more than mortal making ſtars did ſhine,

" That

" That there they cannot but for ever prove
" The monument and pledge of humble love.

The Author of the obfervations on Mr. Waller's
poems, has the following note upon this paffage—
" Thefe verfes apparently refer to fome Tree in
" Penfhurft-park, planted at the birth of the famous
" Sir Philip Sydney, of which there is no tradition
" now remaining in the family; but we may apply
" to it what Cicero fays of the Marian Oak ;"
" *Manet vero, & femper manebit ; fata eft enim ingenio :*
" *nullius autem agricolæ cultu ftirps tam diuturna, quam*
" *poetæ verfu feminari poteft.*"

Ben Johnfon has alfo alluded to this Tree, in his
Foreft, fpeaking of Penfhurft :

Thou haft thy walks for health as well as fport,
Thy mount to which the Druids do refort ;
Where Pan and Bacchus their high feafts have made,
Beneath the broad Beech, and a Chefnut fhade ;
The taller Tree which of a nut was fet
At his great birth, where all the Mufes met.

But whether the Tree was an Oak or a Chefnut,
whether lately felled, or ages ago, fignifies not much :
the anecdote above cited was the occafion of the following little Ode :

E 6   QUERCUS

QUERCUS *loquitur.*

The Oak speaks.

Yes, ye muſt fall, ye fathers of the wood!
Ye, who for ages here have ſtood :
On whom an hundred wintry blaſts have beat,
Who've borne an hundred ſummers heat :
Yes, ye muſt fall, 'tis for your country's good.

The Britiſh Navy ſummons now your aid ;
She calls ;—Oh, be it ever ſaid,
Each Britiſh heart, and ev'ry Britiſh oak,
Looks for the ſignal, waits the ſtroke,
And thinks the ling'ring axe too long delay'd.

Mourn not, ye Nymphs, ye Dryads of the grove,
Mourn not the ſcene of your chaſte love ;
To yon wide-ſpreading ſhades of beech retreat,
There ever fix your ſylvan ſeat,
Where thro' the high-arch'd bow'r the Zephyrs rove.

I, who was planted on the ſacred morn,
On which great Sidney here was born,
With joy exulting quit his once-lov'd plain :
I long to plunge amid the main,
And ſee the Britiſh flag my ſtrength adorn.

And

And thou, well-pleas'd, from thy etherial throne,
Soul of great Sidney, Oh, look down!
Behold the patriot flame that burnt in thee,
Now animates thy honour'd tree,
Who, joyful, meets a death fo like thy own.

Tua Cæfar Ætas. *

ALL, all is Cæfar's, new-rob'd Afton cries,
All, all is Cæfar's, the King's Bench replies.
Poor people, you have nothing left, we fee,
Since all is Cæfar's which belong'd to me.

LIBERTY.

EPISTLE TO MR. CRANMER KENRICK, AT BATH.

AMIDST the pleafures that attend
At Bath, my worthy, honeft friend,
If, unexpected, I intrude,
Forgive me, and not think me rude.

Intent, at firft, my zeal to prove,
And fhew, at once, efteem and love,

* Mr. Juftice Afton's motto upon the rings which he diftri-
buted, upon being made a Judge of the King's Bench.

I thought

I thought, dear Cranmer, to difclofe
My fentiments, in languid profe;
But, gath'ring from acquaintance long,
How much you're fmit with love of fong,
I thought a verfe, as more refin'd,
Would be more grateful, and as kind:
And fo, againft my reafon, chufe,
To pleafe my friend, t' invoke the mufe.

You've read, no doubt, and may admire,
Of country Farmer, and the 'Squire;
How John to London city went,
To fee the 'Squire, and pay his rent;
How 'Squire delighted to behold
His tenant's face, and touch the gold;
Amidft a fet polite and fine,
Wou'd force the farmer into dine—
No perfon can a ftation grace,
Who has not talents for the place—
No wonder then that John is found
The butt and jeft of all around;
For, whilft he tries his wit t' enhance,
With more than ufual complaifance,
He but his want of fenfe difclos'd,
And finds himfelf the more expos'd.

So I, perhaps, with heavy ftuff,
In profe might come off well enough;

But

But ſtriving, void of grace and fear,
To pleaſe, with rhyme, your nicer ear,
May ſhew myſelf the more a fool,
Juſt object of your ridicule.

Oft I revolv'd, devoid of ſtrife,
Th' amuſement of ſcholaſtic life ;
(Bleſt ſtate ! where joy and truth abound,
And pleaſures, void of cares, are found !)
And there the learned page explore,
And con our quondum leſſons o'er :
Or, from the hours of durance free,
To every heart glad liberty ;
Unknown to ſickneſs, care, or pain,
Contend at cricket once again :
Or, bleſt beyond our greateſt hope,
When favour'd with a wider ſcope,
With you, with Bullock, Turner, ſtray,
Where Norwood hills invite the way :
At Allen's, tir'd, ſometimes regale
With wine, or punch, or buns and ale.

Ah ! Turner, much lamented youth,
Adorn'd with Learning, Virtue, Truth !
Had Fate permitted longer ſtay,
Nor ſnatch'd thee from thy friends away,
Thou ſhould'ſt have fill'd ſome nobler place,
Thy country's ornament and grace !

Receive

Receive, thou dear departed fhade,
This tribute to thy mem'ry paid;
And may it, while it fpeaks thy fame,
Tell how I love, revere thy name.

The days of pleafures paft, I wcet,
Are yet in recollection fweet:
Oh! may fucceeding days reflect
A pleafure ftill.in retrofpect;
And leave no bitter thoughts behind,
To ruffle or difturb the mind:
That, when fhall come the final day,
When we the debt of Nature pay,
We may refign without a tear,
Have much to hope, but nought to fear.

The clofing of poor Turner's eyes,
Has led my Mufe to moralize;
Forgive me, if I call anew
His image, Cranmer, to your view,
And caufe you frefhly to deplore
Your friend and mine, alas! no more!

Sometimes, when bufinefs will admit,
I fearch the Regifters of Wit:
To Hiftory I'm often led,
There view the actions of the dead:

By

By this inftructive fcience fhown,
From others faults I learn my own :
Or, to poetic flights inclin'd,
When time permits, and Mufe is kind,
In rhyme I trifle out an hour,
And fing in verfe, of Nature's pow'r :
To love-fick damfels friendly prove,
And fcribble out a cure for Love :
Or, thro' Imagination's aid,
Enraptur'd, court fome painted maid.

Amufements like to thefe I find,
Enlarge th' ideas of the mind ;
Afford more pleafing fweet content,
Than hours of riot, taverns fpent.

Whilft I a vacant hour employ,
To give you pain, or give you joy,
Methinks, with Fancy's airy flight,
I fee you in th' affembly bright,
With eafy, lightfome ftep advance,
Rejoicing in the mazy dance :
Or elfe with Beaux and Belles fit down,
To play at cards for half-a-crown ;
'Till, captiv'd by fome Beauty's art,
You lofe your cafh, or lofe your heart.

I thought

I thought t' enquire your gay defigns,
And health, at firft, in twenty lines :
But foon as e'er I could begin,
Thought upon thought crowding in,
And drove me with fuch rapid force,
I could not eafy ftop my courfe.
So boys in Thames their pleafure take,
One ftep and then another make ;
Till quite depriv'd at length of ftay,
They're carried by the tide away.

But, not to lead you more about,
Nor weary quite your patience out,
If a few minutes you can fpare,
From your attention to the fair,
I fhould be glad to have a letter,
In verfe, or profe if you think better :
How grand the balls, how fine the place,
How gay and fplendid fhines his Grace ;
How Nafh, diverfions all his care,
Affects of youth the fprightly air ;
How hearts to conquer, beauties try,
And throw around th' alluring eye,
To me, if willing, you might fend,
Who am your fervant, and your friend.

JOSEPH MAWBEY.

Vauxhall, April 3, 1753.

ON

ON READING DR. GOLDSMITH'S POEM, THE DESERTED VILLAGE.

BY THE HON. CORBYN MORRIS, ESQ.

Au Contraire. The Reverfe.

MARK the new fcene *, how Wealth and Art unite
T' enrich the foil, and give the eye delight :
Here fhady waftes and rufhy bogs bore fway,
Now fields of corn the ploughman's toil obey,
And lowing paftures cheer the welcome day.
See roads new trac'd for univerfal good,
With ftately bridges to furmount the flood.
The goddefs Culture gains a new domain,
Enliv'ning all, and, with her bufy train,
Spreads a rich mantle over hill and plain :
Whilft Nature views the happy changes made,
With pleafing wonder, like a country maid,
Who, dreft in elegance, with rich array,
Scarce knows herfelf, blufhing to look fo gay.

* Bowood, in Wiltfhire, the feat of the Right Honourable the Earl of Shelburne, &c. &c

THE

THE LOUNGER.

I RISE about nine, get to breakfaſt by ten,
Blow a tune on my flute, or perhaps make a pen ;
Read a play till eleven, or cock my lac'd hat ;
Then ſtep to my neighbour's, till dinner, to chat.
Dinner over, to Tom's or to James's I go,
The news of the town ſo impatient to know ;
While Law, Locke, and Newton, and all the rum race
That talk of their modes, their elipſis, and ſpace,
The ſeat of the ſoul, and new ſyſtems on high,
In holes as abſtruſe as their myſteries, lie.
From the Coffee houſe then to the Tennis away,
And at five I poſt back to my College to pray :
I ſup before eight, and, ſecure fiom all duns,
Undauntedly march to the Mitre, or Tuns ;
Where in punch, or good claret, my ſorrows I drown,
And toſs off a bowl, to the beſt in the town :
At one in the morning I call what's to pay,
Then home to my College I ſtagger away :
Thus I tope all the night, and I trifle all day.

EPISTLE

EPISTLE TO LORD MELCOMBE.

BY RICHARD BENTLEY, ESQ.

I'VE often thought, my Lord, the thing now true,
Said by Lord Bute, but what I've learn'd from you;
" We fhall lofe poetry :" In this alone
Too fhort,—he might have added, " Wit is gone."

How came this prime delight of man thus leffen'd
From its full orb down to a thumb nail crefent ?
With me the cafe admits not of a doubt !
The fact is, poefy itfelf's worn out.
To you, my Lord, this notion I fubmit,
Who knew and help'd to make this age of wit,
Mix'd with thofe demi-gods in verfe and profe,
Congreves, and Addifons, and Garths, and Rowes,
Heroes of giant limb, and high renown,
Whofe deeds we wonder at, and hide our own ;
Whom but to copy in their idle fits,
Would break the backs of puny modern wits.

To fet this matter in the cleareft light,
And be thyfelf th' example while I write,
Let us, my Lord, if fo it may avail,
And you have patience for a long detail,

Give

Give the Earl's fentence a poetic turn;
Let it run thus: " See all Parnaffus mourn,
" Mute ev'ry mufe, fee George's praife unfung,
" Their laurels fcatter'd, and their lyres unftrung,
" Apollo veils with mifts his beamy head,
" Nay, Aganippe murmurs fomething fad."
Say, will this ftile, my Lord, go down or no,
Glib as it did two thoufand years ago?
I fancy fcarce, and favour'd, if it pafs
From a raw fchool-boy in the fecond clafs:
The reafon then why no difguft it drew,
Was, that it might be Truth, for aught they knew.
Thofe early ages no miftruft had fhewn,
Ready their faith, their manners roughly hewn,
And while both Reafon and Sufpicion doz'd,
Prieft, Poet, Prophet, Patriot, impos'd.

With all that either broach'd, the world content,
Believ'd ftill farther than they could invent,
All irrealities came forth reveal'd
By pow'rful Fancy into fact congeal'd.
Then Poetry had elbow-room enough,
And not reftrain'd, as now, for want of ftuff;
The great abyfs of Fable open ftood,
And nothing folid rofe above the flood.

A new Religion fpreading ev'ry where,
The ftock of Poetry fell under par;

For

For Oracles grew dumb, as men grew wife,
None faw for thofe, who faw with their own eyes.
To wafte her leaves no more the fybil choofes,
They and her tripod ferve for other ufes.
No more the Jefuit prompts her what to tell ;
For to fay Middleton and Fontenelle.

But the new doctrines being found too pure,
Some able doctors undertook its cure ;
It ferv'd no purpofes but faving finners,
They added that by which themfelves were winners ;
Ghofts, Devil, Witches, Conjurors, in flocks
Came, like a new fubfcription, to the ftocks ;
And Poetry, enlarg'd with a new range,
Began to fhew her head again in Change.

The world grown old, its youthful follies paft,
Reafon affumes her reign, tho' late, at laft.
By flow degrees, and labouring up the hill,
Step after ftep, yet feeming to ftand ftill,
She wins her way, wherever fhe advances ;
Satyr no more, nor Fawn, nor Dryad dances.
The groves, tho' trembling to a natural breeze,
Difmifs their horrors, and fhew nought but trees.
Before her, Nonfenfe, Superftition fly ;
We burn no Witch, let her be e'er fo dry :
A woman now may live, tho' paft her prime,
So hallow'd and fo gracious is the time.

Bankrupt

Bankrupt of deities, with all their train,
And set to work without his tools in vain,
Not genius-crampt (but what can genius do
When it's tied down to one and one make two?)
How can poor Poet ſtir? In ſuch a caſe
We muſt do ſomething to ſupply their place.

See, at his beck, all Nouns renouncing ſenſe,
Start into perſons of ſome conſequence.
Proud of new being, tread poetic ground,
And aggregate their attributes around;
Theſe he may uſe of right, as his own growth,
In all the reſt confin'd to ſober Truth.

To bleſs a nation, ſee Charlotta come,
'Twas Anſon, and not Neptune, brought her home.
A ſingle Nereid ſtirr'd not from below,
The duce a conch did e'er one Triton blow;
But, in revenge ſhe plough'd her ſubject main,
With every virtue 'tending in her train.
Hark, 'tis a people's univerſal voice,
That bleſs, while they approve their Sov'reign's choice.

On ſuch a theme, my Lord, might one extend
Far as one would, nor ſtricteſt Truth offend,
'Twere only proper epithets to find,
To every grace of perſon and of mind;

With

With decent dress, and emblem to improve
All that can merit our esteem and love.
But then to Poetry where's the pretence?
Locke and Sir Isaac write not plainer sense.
From the first ages down to modern time,
Derive the pleasing stream of verse and rhime,
However vast from its first source it rose,
Th' inverted river dwindles as it flows.

Thus from the lunar hills some other Nile,
Swoln with new stores from snows that melt the while,
Stretches his current on to fiercer suns,
And glads a thousand nations as he runs,
Till having reach'd, proud of his long career,
Those sands which belt the middle of our sphere,
Exhal'd, absorb'd, diverted, dry foot cross'd,
And, finger'd into rivulets, is lost.

Fall'n cherub Simile, who erst divine,
Cloath'd with transcendant beauty didst outshine;
Plain angel Poesy, how art thou lost!
Sunk in Oblivion's pit! from what height toss'd!

Thus to plain Narrative confin'd alone,
Figure, Description, Simile quite gone;
The whole affair evinc'd which we contend,
The thing has had its day, and there's an end.

With Milton, Epic drew its lateſt breath,
Since Shakeſpeare, Tragedy puts us to death ;
Th' aſſaſſin Satire ſheaths the keen ſtiletto,
And languiſhes, depriv'd of the Concetto ;
The age with pious eye no longer views
The great mortality of groſs abuſe.

Soft Elegy has dried up all her tears,
And Gray compoſes once in ſeven years ;
Celia's and Delia's ſhine no more in ſong,
Nor ballad bauls the deafen'd ſtreets along.

My Lord, a little patience further ſtill,
To " Wit is gone," by way of codicil ;
Who but will ſay the thing that hears me tell ?—
The man miſtakes—Lord Melcombe's very well,
Suppoſe I ſaid—O could I! War is done,
Means it there's no ſuch thing, as ſword, or gun ?
Party and Faction dead, whoever grants,
Means he that every man has what he wants ?
In all theſe caſes is implied alone,
That there's no object to employ them on.

A Court, my Lord, and Miniſter to hit,
And cry corruption, make all public wit :
'Tis on this ſenſe my reaſon chiefly ſtands—
There may be caſh enough in private hands.

Now

Now where could Malice bite, or Envy sting,
The polish'd model of a perfect King?
Of Ministers what mighty matters tell?
They give, we know, but neither buy nor sell.

Add we to what we've said, this little more,
That all that can be wrote, is wrote before;
That pool of knowledge fish'd, poach'd, dragg'd and
     drain'd,
Till nothing bigger than a grig remain'd;
And painful writers think it a good day,
If they can hook a news-paper essay,
And must remain so till blank years of grace,
Suspending future writing, shall take place;
Put down our piddling, bobbing, and allow
The spawn and fry of Science time to grow.

But while we're on this subject, 'tis worth thinking,
How little salt has kept this world from stinking;
'Tis the same wit, at different times alive,
Sunk at Whitehall, to rise up at Queenhithe.

Born in whatever clime, whatever age,
We trace it first from the Athenian stage,
Where Liberty a little licence claim'd,
There, just as somewhere else, that shan't be nam'd;
Taught all her sons this fav'rite to adore,
Much for itself, because abusive more;

For

For every comic writer braided it,
Two threads of Scandal to one thread of Wit :
O'er all, fee Ariftophanes prefide,
And flafh his lightnings round on every fide,
Struck the fham patriot, the fwoln Poet wafted,
Alas ! e'en Socrates himfelf he blafted.

What was the burft directly over head,
So loud its echo, now its fires fo red,
Tho' oft thro' Time's thick cloud the trembling gleam
We only catch, but mifs the vivid beam ;
While half-feen thoughts, like meteors, twinkle light,
And draw their lucid trails athwart the night.

Hither, unto their fountain, other ftars
Repairing, fwell their own peculiars,
By tincture or reflection ; Lucian hence,
His golden urn replenifh'd ; and long fince
Rabelais from both his urinal drew full ;
From him, and them, Swift crowded his clofe-ftool.
Howe'er it came, with the ftrange paffion ftung,
To raife his choiceft fruit on rankeft dung ;
Fully convinc'd his jeffamine and rofe
Smelt fweeteft, planted by his little houfe :
Yet ftill fome cleaner parts diftinguifh'd lay,
Like cherry-ftones upon a child's C— C—

The

The nasty lines, my Lord, demand excuse,
Happ'ly the times are free from that abuse :
Our descent manners all obscenness flout,
And Wit is at one entrance quite shut out.

From hence, my Lord, Wit took a tour about,
Residing in few countries on his rout,
Appear'd in places, but ne'er took his seat in
One spot of earth, except Greece, France, and Britain.
The rest a single trophy only bear,
And just enough to show he had been there.
As Nature's ideot never fails to hit,
Once in his life, on some sheer strokes of Wit ;
Then stoops ten thousand fathoms down behind,
Plump in his own vacuity of mind,
A like excursion never to repeat
To the warm regions of ætherial heat.
Yet when we look at home, my Lord, at best,
We find but little that will stand the test ;
But then the boasted days of Charles the Second,
Unless Debauchery for Wit is reckon'd,
Most that they had appears, by looking back,
A fungus growing on their butt of sack.
E'en my good cousin Rochester's but barren,
From wholesome meat if you deduct the carrion.

In the next reigns how could it flourish much ?
Bigotry, Revolution, and the Dutch.

Damp'd,

Damp'd, like wet blankets, its aspiring flame,
And if not quite extinguish'd, kept it tame,
Till orient Anna lighted all its fires,
And the glad stars responsive tun'd their choirs;
Pity she e'er left any in the lurch,
To follow those who lighted her to church.

    Then Halifax, my Lord, as you do yet,
Stood forth the friend of Poetry and Wit;
Sought silent Merit in its secret cell,
And Heav'n, nay even man repaid him well.
Man, in the praise of every grateful quill,
And Heav'n in him, who bears his title still:
Who, on a kingdom to his virtues won,
Reflects the glories of our British Sun.

THE late Lord E—g—e was not only a man of
pleasure, but of fine parts, great knowledge, and
original wit.—In him we have the most affecting example, how health, fame, ambition, every thing, are
drawn into that most destructive of all whirlpools—
gaming. No man was ever more calculated by nature to serve the public, and charm society—I shall
leave the shades of this picture unfinished, as, perhaps, they were not wholly owing to his own indis-
cretion, but his F——'s rigor. To give an idea of
his

his light, eafy vein of wit and poetry, we fhall prefent the reader with the following fable, well known
to be written by him, and never publifhed before.

FABLE OF THE ASS, NIGHTINGALE, AND KID.

BY THE LATE LORD E———.

——*Trahit fua quemq; voluptas.*

ONCE on a time it came to pafs,
A Nightingale, a Kid, and Afs,
A Jack one, all fet out together,
Upon a trip—no matter whither;
And thro' a village chanc'd to take
Their journey—where there was a wake;
With lads and laffes all affembled:
Our travellers, whofe genius them led
Each his own way—refolv'd to tafte
Their fhare o'th' fport—we're not in hafte,
Firft cries the Nightingale, and I
Delight in mufic mightily!
Let's have a tune—ay, come, let's ftop,
Replied the Kid, and take a hop.
Ay, do, fays Jack, the mean while I
Will wait for you, and graze hard by.
You know that I, for fong and dance,
Care not a fart—but if, by chance,
As probably the end will be,
They go a romping—then call me.

F 4

SEATED

SEATED one day in a warm bofom of hills, covered with evergreens, with a fmall trout ftream running through the middle, I reflected on the fafhion of Englifhmen repairing to Nice, in Piedmont, for the eftablifhment of health, as arifing more from the love of change in general, than to anfwer any falutary purpofes. The accounts of the remarkable inclemency of the feafon at that place, and the death of two men of confequence, gave rife to the following lines.

ODE TO HEALTH.

WRITTEN MARCH 10, 1775.

IN vain ye feek the warmer fky,
   Where Var * rolls down her Alpine tide,
And flow'rs unfold their varied dye,
   In earlier fragrance by its fide :
Yet whom a length of well-fpent years deprefs,
Or wanton lives whofe complicated ills confefs.

Dowdefwell in vain invok'd the maid,
   Or on the hill, or milder dale ;
But found her not amid the glade,
   Nor caught her in the whifpering gale ;

* A river that rifes in the Alps, and runs by Nice.

There

There—but such loss what time will see supplied!
Britons, your truest, firmest patriot genius died.

For lo ! with wreath fantastic crown'd,
   She treads this solitary scene ;
And lightly trips these woodlands round,
   Bedeck'd with stole of vernal green ;
Glides gently down the murmuring stream below,
And tempers with her pow'r the rougher winds that
   blow.

From youth, thee, rustic nymph, I woo'd,
   At ev'ning grey, and crimson morn,
Thy steps on beds of violets view'd,
   And saw thee wanton on the thorn.
Far more, the humble shrub and poorer cell,
Thou lov'st than in th' intemp'rate air of courts to
   dwell.

But tho' thy influence benign
   To me produce unclouded days,
Yet true Contentment is not mine,
   Unless you claim my Laura's praise,
And bid her blood with livelier impulse flow,
And on her pallid cheek the banish'd roses glow.

F 5

From grief she rescues the oppress'd,
    And drops the sympathetic tear;
She pours her balm into the breast
    Of virtuous indigence and care.
'Thus from corroding fear and want set free,
She bids them Heav'n address—then sacrifice to thee.

AN EPIGRAM

ON A CERTAIN LADY'S COMING INTO THE ROOM AT BATH, WITH A DIAMOND CRESCENT IN HER HAIR.

BY MR. POTTER.

CHASTE Dian's crescent on her front display'd,
Behold! the wife proclaims herself a maid!
Come, fierce Taillard, or fiercer Junius come,
On this fair subject urge the contest home;
Pluck honour from this emblematic moon,
And solve the point which puzzles Warburton:
This radiant emblem you may then transpose,
And give the horned crescent to the spouse.

BY E. D——X, ESQ. ON HIS DAUGHTER'S BIRTH-
DAY.

THE twenty-fecond day of May
Is little Fanny's natal day;
Pretty warblers of the wood,
Quit awhile your callow brood,
Gaily prune each gaudy wing,
Each a merry carol bring,
To commemorate the morn,
When my little maid was born.

Come, Aurora! bring thy hours,
All array'd in May-morn flowers;
Ev'ry hour fhall wear a fmile,
Little troubles to beguile;
Airy phantoms, lightly tread
O'er the cowflip's glittering head,
O'er the cup of golden hue,
Fill'd this morn with filver dew,
By kind Nature fill'd for you;
Let each little fairy lip,
Of the pearly dew-drop fip,
Nature pours out all her wealth,
Drink to her's and Fanny's health;
She, I'm fure, will not refufe,
Gratefully thofe gifts to ufe.

F 6   O Inno-

O Innocence! protect her Youth,
Lead her down the paths of Truth,
Culling sweets from every flower,
Truth has twin'd round Virtue's bower,
There to dwell with sweet Content,
Virtue's constant resident.

Sweets too redolent will cloy;
Prudence mildly tempers joy;
Thorns may grow tho' sweets are near,
Pity oft will have her tear;
Tears will start, howe'er confin'd,
From a feeling generous mind.

Idleness for ever meets
Bitter, in its cup of sweets!
Let her not recline her head,
Long on Pleasure's rosy bed,
Pleasure does itself destroy,
Be improvement then her toy,
Doing right her greatest joy.
Mindful of her parent's nod,
And her duty to her God;
Tell her " to the good and wise,
" Every place is paradise;
" Every month to them is May,
" And a birth-day every day."

ON BREAKING A CHINA QUART MUG BELONGING
TO THE SOCIETY OF LINCOLN COLLEGE,
OXFORD.

BY AN UNDER GRADUATE.

O D E.

Amphora non meruit tam pretiofa mori.

I.

WHENE'ER the cruel hand of Death
Untimely ftops a fav'rite's breath,
Mufes in plaintive numbers tell
How lov'd he liv'd—how mourn'd he fell:
Catullus 'wail'd his fparrow's fate,
And Gray immortaliz'd his cat.
Thrice tuneful bards! could I but chime fo clever,
My Quart, my honeft Quart, fhould live for ever.

II.

How weak is all a mortal's pow'r,
T'avert the death-devoted hour!
Nor can a fhape, or beauty fave,
From the fure conqueft of the grave.

In vain the butler's choiceſt care,
   The maſter's wiſh, the burſer's pray'r !
For when life's lengthen'd to its longeſt ſpan,
China itſelf muſt fall, as well as Man.

III.

   Can I forget how oft my Quart
     Has ſooth'd my care, and warm'd my heart ?
   When barley lent its balmy aid,
     And all its liquid charms diſplay'd !
   When orange and the nut-brown toaſt
     Swam mantling round the ſpicey coaſt !
The pleaſing depth I view'd with ſparkling eyes,
Nor envied Jove the nectar of the ſkies.

IV.

   The fide-board, on that fatal day,
   When you in glitt'ring ruins lay,
   Mourn'd at thy loſs—in guggling tone,
   Decanters poured out their moan—
   A dimneſs hung on ev'ry glaſs—
   Joe * wonder'd what the matter was—
Corks ſelf contracted free'd the frantic beer,
And ſympathizing tankards dropt a tear.

* The college butler.

V. Where

V.

Where are the flow'ry wreaths that bound
In rofy rings thy chaplets round?
The azure ftars whofe glitt'ring rays
Promis'd a happier length of days!
The trees that on thy border grew,
And bloffom'd with eternal blue!
Trees, ftars and flow'rs are fcatter'd on the floor,
And all thy brittle beauties are no more.—

VI.

Hadft thou been form'd of coarfer earth,
Had Nottingham but giv'n thee birth!
Or had thy variegated fide
Of Stafford's fable hue been dy'd,
Thy ftately fabric had been found,
Tho' tables tumbled on the ground.—
The fineft mould the fooneft will decay;
Hear this, ye Fair, for you yourfelves are clay!

N

ON SEEING THE BEAUTIFUL MISS CHARLOTTE
COLLINS, OF WINCHESTER, COPY A DRAWING
OF THE JUDGMENT OF PARIS.

O matre pulchrâ, filia pulchrior !

HOW true the mimic forms appear,
The ebon fhield and glitt'ring fpear !
The piercing eye, the fteady mien,
As erft in Athens fhe was feen ;
Or rifing from her borrow'd guife,
She ftruck th' aftonifh'd * Grecian's eyes.
And in celeftial radiance dreft,
The martial goddefs ftood confeft.

With brow indignant and fevere,
See Juno, jealous Queen, appear ;
Stern, as when flighted by her God,
She made Heav'n tremble at her nod.
But thefe are Fancy's airy train,
That fir'd old Homer's epic ftrain ;
Made heroes fight and deities jar,
And kept alive a ten years war.

* When Minerva had conducted Telemachus to Ithaca, under
the appearance of Old Mentor, fhe refumed her form and left him.

Charlotte,

Charlotte, thy pencil's fkill'd to trace
Superior forms and eàfier grace :
Why copy then what Fiction drew,
When Nature holds herfelf to view !
Ceafe on this Cyprian form to gaze,
And truft thy faithful mirror's rays ;
By its reflected aid, you'll know
More vivid tints, the warmer glow.
The auburn ringlet—brilliant eye—
Dimples—where Loves in ambufh lie—
Teeth—as the Ceylon ivory white—
Lips—with the Perfian coral dight—
The graceful neck—and fwelling breaft—
Here Fancy blufhing paints the reft.

FUSEE, R. G. R.

Dec. 1778.

INSCRIBED WITHIN A TOWER WHICH MAKES
PART OF A RUINED CASTLE, ERECTED LATELY
AT WIMPOLE, THE SEAT OF THE EARL OF
HARDWICKE, IN CAMBRIDGESHIRE.

BY DANIEL WRAY, ESQ.

WHEN * Henry ftemm'd Ierne's ftormy flood,
And bow'd to Britain's yoke her favage brood ;

* Henry II.

When

When by true courage and falfe zeal impell'd,
* Richard encamp'd on Salem's palmy field ;
On towers like thefe, Earl, Baron, Vavafor,
Hung high their banners waving in the air ;
Free, hardy, proud, they brav'd their feudal Lord,
And tried their rights by ordeal of the fword ;
Now the full board with Chriftmas plenty crown'd ;
Now ravag'd and opprefs'd the country round ;
Yet Freedom's caufe once rais'd the civil broil,
And Magna Charta clos'd the glorious toil.

Spruce modern villas different fcenes afford
The Patriot Baronet, the Courtier Lord,
Gently amus'd now wafte the Summer's day,
In *Book-room*, *Print-room*, or in *Ferme Ormée* :
While wit, champaign, and pines and poetry,
Virtù and ice the genial feaft fupply.
But hence the poor are cherifh'd, artifts fed,
And Vanity relieves—in Bounty's ftead.

Oh! might our age in happy concert join
The manly virtues of the Norman line,
With the true fcience and juft tafte which raife
High in each ufeful art thefe modern days !

* Richard I.

A MO;

A MODERN INVOCATION TO A COOK-MAID.

BY MR. K——, OF K— COL. C——E.

Ne fit ancillæ tibi amor pudori,
———prius infolentem,
Serva Brifcis niveo colore
Movit Achillem.   **HOR.**

COME and crown your lover's wifhes,
    Vain's the tafk you now purfue,
Leave, ah leave, your pewter difhes,
    Think not they can fhine like you.

Though no borrow'd airs befriend you,
    Carelefs Beauty wins the heart;
And if Nature's fmells attend you,
    Health is fweeter far than Art.

What tho' curling fteams around thee,
    Quick in circling eddies play,
Beauty's luftre would confound me,
    Did not that obfcure its ray.

While you fcrub that radiant pewter,
    That reflects your rofy hue,
Who'd not wifh to be a fuitor,
    To its bright reflection too.

What

What tho' low and mean your place is,
Still you fhine with native pride,
And your rags difcover graces,
Which brocades would only hide.

A POETICAL EPISTLE TO LORD KELLY, OCCA-
SIONED BY HIS MIRACULOUS ESCAPE FROM
SHIPWRECK, IN THE PASSAGE FROM CALAIS
TO DOVER, DURING THE GREAT STORM IN
NOVEMBER 1775.

" *Illi Robur et æs triplex
Circa Pectus erat, qui fragilem truci
Commifit Pelago ratem ;——
Qui ficcis occulis Monftra Natantia
Qui vidit Mare Turgidum !*"

HORAT. ODE 3,

DARK was the day, the wind rag'd high,
Black roll'd the clouds athwart the fky,
Sublime was heard the thunder's roar,
Re-echoing from fhore to fhore :
The rain in floods the foreft bath'd,
The tow'ring oaks the light'ning fcath'd,
While fpectres dire of horrid form
Clung to the wild wings of the ftorm.

Such

Such was the time when Kelly's Lord
The Calais Pacquet ftepp'd aboard;
The Peer difplay'd a flufh of face,
That might a Paris Duchefs grace,
Embofom'd deep in ev'ry dimple,
There fiery gleam'd a purple pimple,
Like Summer cloud that lightning vomits,
Or fkies at night that blaze with comets;
Curious with carbuncle and ruby,
Not like a whey-fac'd milk-fop booby,
That looks inanimate and filly,
And languid as a drooping lilly:
No—the red grape, or damafk'd rofe,
Vivid upon his vifage glows;
His jolly countenance look'd big,
All elegant with Gallic wig,
To decorate the head of Earl,
Wig ne'er difplay'd fo fweet a curl;
All other wigs to this muft truckle,
And hide in *papillotes* their buckle;
A compofition rich and rare,
Pomatum, fcented-powder, hair:
" *A combination and a form*"
Might foften rocks, or calm a ftorm!
Such was the wig, and fuch the curl;—
When lo! the tars the fails unfurl,
Light o'er the billows bounds the fkiff,
And fhapes her courfe tow'rds Dover Cliff.

Mean

Mean time the gale blows loud and ftrong,
Mix'd with the fcreaming Curlew's fong;
The ftorm with ten-fold fury raves,
And fwells to tumult all the waves;
Still thro' the wild, impetuous furges,
All defperate her way fhe urges,
And proudly fwims a very duck,
Till on a a fhelving fand fhe ftruck:
Each paffenger with terror faints,
Pale fear each rueful vifage paints,
They tremble left they find a pillow
In each obftrep'rous dafhing billow;
The mind of Kelly fpurns at Fate,
Collected all, and all fedate,
He bears for bravery and the palm,
All ftorm without, within all calm.
Tho' ev'ry hair hangs loofe and lank,
Or like fome weeping willow dank;
Altho' his wig be drench'd with brine,
He fcorns ignobly to repine.——
Such courage charms the pow'rs above,
So off again the bark they fhove;
Green Nereids gaily round her fport,
And point the way to Dover's port;
The drooping crew with fongs they footh,
And all the ruffled deep they fmooth;
The moon reftrains the fwelling tides,
The howling hurricane fubfides.

In

In ancient ſtory thus I've found,
That no Muſician e'er was drown'd;
A harp was then, or I miſtake it,
Much better than the beſt cork-jacket;
The Grecian harpers went abroad,
The lockers well with liquor ſtor'd;
For harpers ever had a thirſt,
Since harping was invented firſt.
They in the cabbin ſat a drinking,
Till the poor ſhip was almoſt ſinking;
Then running nimbly to the poop,
They gave the ſcaly brood a whoop;
And, ſudden as they form'd the wiſh,
For ev'ry harper came a fiſh;
Then o'er the briny billows ſcudding,
They car'd for drowning not a pudding.—
Methinks, my Lord, with cheek of roſe,
I ſee you mount your bottle noſe;
Or firmly holding by a whole fin,
Ride degagé upon your dolphin.

'Twas thus the tuneful Peer of Kelly
Eſcap'd ſome whale's enormous belly;
And, ſafe in London thinks no longer,
He'll prove a feaſt for ſhark or conger.

A. E.

ON THE LADIES FEATHERS.

Quid vento levius? Pulvis. Quid pulvere? Pluma.
Quid pluma? Mulier. Quid muliere? Nihil.

Dust's lighter than the wind—than dust a feather;
But Woman's lighter than all these together.

THE Ladies have brought in feathers again with the Winter and the woodcocks. The Philosopher's description of an human creature, *animal bipes implume*, " a two-legg'd, unfeathered animal," is no longer applicable to our women; and the men have nothing to do, in order to destroy the definition on their part, but to follow Rousseau's system, and to walk upon all-fours.

The female sex seem at present to wish to be considered as a collection of all the birds in the air. Some few sing in a cage; many entertain us with their wild notes: and most of them give us to understand, that any violence offered to them, is a kind of petty-offence, not so punishable as robbing a hen-roost.

In complaisance to the Ladies, I have sometimes amused myself with following the train in which

they

they have appeared defirous to lead us. When I fee the black feathers of a widow, I confider them as emblems of the plumes nodding over the hearfe of her late hufband, confequently as a notice that there is room for another; and when I behold the white feathers on the head of an unmarried Lady, I interpret them as the triumph of a young innocent on being juft fledged, or, perhaps, as an intimation from fome more knowing fair one, of the deceafe of her virginity. The high top of a ftately Woman of Quality in the fide-box, has more than once reminded me of the peacock; while the fhawls and varied plumage of the Eaft India Directors' Ladies in the front, have brought to my imagination the idea of Chinefe peafants and Bantams. The female *birds of prey* in other parts of the Theatre, with their keen eyes, have put me in mind of hawks, eagles, and vultures; and the more common fort in the greenboxes, I have compared to *Guinea* hens; and upon feeing Prince Orlow at the play, fome time ago, while I was indulging thefe fpeculations, I could not help thinking of his gallant miftrefs, who is faid to have a ftomach capable of digefting lead and iron, and of courfe refembling her to an oftrich.

Having once fallen into this vein, it is impoffible to go to a route, or into any numerous affembly, without converting the feathers of the daughters of goffipping, fcandal, and chit-chat, into marks of cuckows, parrots and magpies. When I go to the Opera, and obferve the plumes and the performers, the Gabrielli—*cum femiviro comitatu*—appears like a nightingale furrounded by capons. But when I turn to the boxes, I cannot but agree, that if there is one woman who is acknowledged to be a good wife, a good mother, and a good friend, fuch a woman ought to be confidered as the Bird of Paradife.

Bird-ftreet.   ORNITHOLOGOS.

A PRAYER TO INDIFFERENCE.

BY MRS. GREVILLE.

OFT I've implor'd the Gods in vain,
    And pray'd till I've been weary;
For once I'll ftrive my wifh to gain,
    Of Oberon, the Fairy.

Sweet airy being, wanton fprite,
    Who liv'ft in woods unfeen,
And oft by Cynthia's filver light
    Trips gaily o'er the green;

If

If e'er thy pitying heart was mov'd,
    (As ancient ſtories tell)
And for th' Athenian maid, who lov'd,
    Thou ſought'ſt a wond'rous ſpell.

Oh! deign once more t' exert thy pow'r;
    Haply ſome herb or tree,
Sov'reign as juice from weſtern flow'r,
    Conceals a balm for me.

I aſk no kind return in love,
    No tempting charm to pleaſe;
Far from that heart ſuch gifts remove,
    Which ſighs for peace and eaſe.

Nor eaſe, nor peace, that heart can know,
    That, like the needle true,
Turns at the touch of joy or woe,
    But, turning, trembles too.

For as diſtreſs the ſoul can wound,
    'Tis plain in each degree,
Bliſs goes but to a certain bound,
    Beyond, 'tis agony.

Then take this treacherous ſenſe of mine,
    Which dooms me ſtill to ſmart:
Which Pleaſure can to Pain refine,
    To Pain new pangs impart!

Oh!

Oh! hafte to fhade the fov'reign balm,
　　My fhatter'd nerves new ftring;
And for my gueft, ferenely calm,
　　The nymph, Indifference, bring.

At her approach, fee Hope, fee Fear,
　　See Expectation fly;
With Difappointment in the rear,
　　That blaft the purpos'd joy.

The tears which Pity taught to flow,
　　My eyes fhall then difown;
The heart which throbb'd for others woe,
　　Shall then fcarce feel its own.

The wounds which now each moment bleed,
　　Each moment then fhall clofe;
And peaceful days fhall ftill fucceed
　　To nights of fweet repofe.

Oh, Fairy Elf! but grant me this,
　　This one kind comfort fend;
And fo may never-fading blifs
　　Thy flow'ry paths attend!

So may the glow-worm's glimmering light
　　Thy tiny footfteps lead,
To fome new region of delight,
　　Unknown to mortal tread!

And

And be the acorn-goblet fill'd
  With Heav'n's ambrosial dew,
From sweetest, freshest flow'rs distill'd,
  That shed fresh sweets for you.

And what of life remains for me
  I'll pass in sober ease;
Half-pleas'd, contented will I be,
  Content but half to please.

TWO LOVE ELEGIES.

Argel itanas mavis habitare Tabernas,
  Cum tibi, parve liber, scrinia nostra vacent.
Nescis, heu! nescis dominæ Fastidia Romæ:
  Crede mihi, nimium martia turba sapit.
Ætherias, lascive, cupis volitare per auras:
  I, fuge; sed poteras tutior esse domi.   MARTIAL.

ELEGY I.

'TIS night, dead night; and o'er the plain
  Darkness extends her ebon ray,
While wide along the gloomy scene
  Deep Silence holds her solemn sway;

G 3

Through-

Throughout the Earth no chearful beam
   The melancholy eye furveys,
Save where the world's fantaftic gleam
   The 'nighted traveller betrays.
The favage race (fo Heav'n decrees)
   No longer thro' the foreft rove ;
All Nature refts, and not a breeze
   Difturbs the ftillnefs of the grove :
All Nature refts ; in Sleep's foft arms
   The village fwain forgets his care :
Sleep, that the fting of Sorrow charms,
   And heals all fadnefs but Defpair ;
Defpair, alone, her power denies ;
   And, when the Sun withdraws his rays,
To the wild beach diftracted flies,
   Or, chearlefs, through the defart ftrays :
Or, to the church-yard's horrors led,
   While fearful echoes burft around,
On fome cold ftone he leans his head,
   Or throws his body on the ground.
To fome fuch drear and folemn fcene,
   Some friendly power direct my way,
Where pale Misfortune's haggard train,
   Sad luxury ! delights to ftray :
Wrapp'd in the folitary gloom,
   Retir'd from Life's fantaftic crew,
Refign'd, I'll wait my final doom,
   And bid the bufy world adieu.

                              The

The world has now no joy for me :
    Nor can life, now, one pleasure boast ;
Since all my eyes desired to see,
    My wish, my hope, my all is lost :
Since she, so form'd to please and bless,
    So wise, so innocent, so fair,
Whose converse sweet made Sorrow less,
    And brighten'd all the gloom of care :
Since she is lost—ye powers divine !
    What have I done, or thought, or said ?
O say ! what horrid act of mine,
    Has drawn this vengeance on my head ?
Why should Heaven favour Lycon's claim ?
    Why are my heart's best wishes crost ?
What fairer deeds adorn his name ?
    What nobler merits can he boast ?
What higher worth in him was found,
    My true heart's service to outweigh ?
A senseless fop !—a dull compound
    Of scarcely animated clay !
He dress'd indeed, he danc'd with ease,
    And charm'd her, by repeating o'er
Unmeaning raptures in her praise,
    That twenty fools had said before :
But I, alas ! who thought all art
    My passion's force would meanly prove,
Could only boast an honest heart,
    And claim'd no merit but my love.

Have

Have I not fate—ye confcious hours,
   Be witnefs—while my Stella fu ng,
From morn to eve, with all my powers
   Wrapt in th' enchantment of her tongue!
Ye confcious hours, that faw me ftand,
   Entranc'd in wonder and furprize,
In filent rapture prefs her hand,
   With paffion burfting from my eyes.
Have I not lov'd ?—O Earth and Heaven!
   Where, now, is all my youthful boaft ?
The dear exchange I hop'd was giv'n
   For flighted Fame, and Fortune loft !
Where now the joys that once were mine ?
   Where all my hopes of future blifs ?
Muft I thofe joys, thofe hopes, refign ?
   Is all her friendfhip come to this ?
Muft then, each woman faithlefs prove ;
   And each fond lover be undone ?
Are vows no more !—Almighty Love !
   The fad remembrance let me fhun !
It will not be—my honeft heart
   The dear, fad image ftill retains ;
And fpite of Reafon, fpite of Art,
   The dreadful memory remains.
Ye Powers divine, whofe wondrous fkill
   Deep in the womb of Time can fee,
Behold, I bend me to your will,
   Nor dare arraign your high decree !

Let

Let her be blefs'd with health, with eafe,
　　With all your bounty has in ftore;
Let forrow cloud my future days,
　　Be Stella bleft !—I afk no more.
But lo ! where high in yonder Eaft,
　　The ftar of Morning mounts apace !
Hence—let me fly th' unwelcome gueft,
　　And bid the Mufe's labour ceafe.

ELEGY II.

WHEN young, Life's journey I began,
　　The glittering profpeft charm'd my eyes,
I faw along th' extended plain
　　Joy after joy fucceffive rife :
And Fame her golden trumpet blew ;
　　And Power difplay'd her gorgeous charms ;
And Wealth engag'd my wandering view ;
　　And Pleafure woo'd me to her arms :
To each, by turns, my vows I paid,
　　As Folly led me to admire ;
While Fancy magnified each fhade,
　　And Hope encreas'd each fond defire.
But foon I found 'twas all a dream ;
　　And learn'd the fond purfuit to fhun,
Where few can reach their purpos'd aim,
　　And thoufands, daily, are undone :

And

And Fame, I found, was empty air;
   And Wealth had terror for her gueſt;
And Pleaſure's path was ſtrew'd with Care;
   And Power was vanity at beſt.
Tir'd of the chace, I gave it o'er;
   And, in a far ſequeſter'd ſhade,
To Contemplation's ſober power
   My youth's next ſervices I paid.
There Health and Peace adorn'd the ſcene;
   And oft, indulgent to my prayer,
With mirthful eye, and frolic mien,
   The Muſe would deign to viſit there:
There would ſhe oft, delighted, rove
   The flow'r-enamell'd vale along;
Or wander with me through the grove,
   And liſten to the wood-lark's ſong;
Or, 'mid the foreſt's awful gloom,
   Whilſt wild amazement fill'd my eyes,
Recall paſt ages from the tomb,
   And bid ideal worlds ariſe.
Thus, in the Muſe's favour bleſt,
   One wiſh alone my ſoul could frame,
And Heaven beſtow'd, to crown the reſt,
   A friend, and Thyrſis was his name.
For manly conſtancy, and truth,
   And worth, unconſcious of a ſtain,
He bloom'd, the flower of Britain's youth,
   The boaſt and wonder of the plain.

                              Still,

Still, with our years, our friendſhip grew;
　　No cares did then my peace deſtroy:
Time brought new bleſſings, as he flew;
　　And every hour was wing'd with joy:
But ſoon the bliſsful ſcene was loſt;
　　Soon did the ſad reverſe appear;
Love came, like an untimely froſt,
　　To blaſt the promiſe of my year.
I ſaw young Daphne's angel form,
　　(Fool that I was, I bleſt the ſmart)
And, while I gaz'd, nor thought of harm,
　　The dear infection ſeiz'd my heart:
She was—at leaſt in Damon's eyes—
　　Made up of lovelineſs and grace;
Her heart a ſtranger to diſguiſe;
　　Her mind as perfect as her face;
To hear her ſpeak, to ſee her move,
　　(Unhappy I, alas! the while)
Her voice was joy, her look was love,
　　And Heaven was open in her ſmile!
She heard me breathe my am'rous prayers,
　　She liſten'd to the tender ſtrain,
She heard my ſighs, ſhe ſaw my tears,
　　And ſeem'd, at length, to ſhare my pain.
She ſaid ſhe lov'd—and I, poor youth!
　　(How ſoon, alas! can Hope perſuade!)
Thought all ſhe ſaid no more than truth,
　　And all my love was well repaid.

Iв

In joys unknown to Courts, or Kings,
   With her I fate the live-long day,
And faid and look'd fuch tender things,
   As none befide could look, or fay!
How foon can Fortune fhift the fcene,
   And all our earthly blifs deftroy?—
Care hovers round, and Grief's fell train
   Still treads upon the heels of Joy.
My age's hope, my youth's beft boaft,
   My foul's chief bleffing, and my pride,
In one fad moment all were loft;
   And Daphne chang'd, and Thyrfis died.
Oh, who, that heard her vows ere-while,
   Could dream thofe vows were infincere?
Or, who could think, that faw her fmile,
   That Fraud could find admittance there?
Yet, fhe was falfe!—my heart will break!
   Her frauds her perjuries were fuch—
Some other tongue than mine muft fpeak—
   I have not power to fay how much!
Ye fwains, hence warn'd, the bait avoid;
   Oh fhun her paths, the trait'refs fhun!
Her voice is death, her fmile is fate,
   Who hears, or fees her, is undone.
And, when Death's hand fhall clofe my eye,
   (For foon, I know, the day will come)
Oh chear my fpirit with a figh;
   And grave thefe lines upon my tomb.

THE EPITAPH.

CONSIGN'D to duſt, beneath this ſtone,
  In manhood's pride is Damon laid;
Joyleſs he liv'd, and died unknown,
  In bleak Misfortune's barren ſhade.
Lov'd by the Muſe, but lov'd in vain—
  'Twas Beauty drew his ruin on;
He ſaw young Daphne on the plain ;
  He lov'd, believ'd, and was undone :
His heart then ſunk beneath the ſtorm,
  (Sad meed of unexampled truth)
And Sorrow, like an envious worm,
  Devour'd the bloſſom of his youth.
Beneath this ſtone the youth is laid—
  Oh greet his aſhes with a tear !
May Heaven with bleſſings crown his ſhade.
  And grant that peace he wanted here !

STANZAS TO ————, WITH THE FOREGOING
ELEGIES.

SINCE you permit the lowly Muſe
  This offering at your feet to lay,
Her flight with ardour ſhe renews ;
  Nor heeds the perils of the way :

If,

If, in the Poet's artless lays,
   Late warbled in his native grove,
You find, perchance, one line to praife,
   Or fhould one fentiment approve;
Let critics babble o'er and o'er,
   Of figures falfe, and accent wrong.
Bleft in thy fmile he afks no more—
   There muft be merit in the fong.
But, when of Epitaph and Worm,
   Of Death and Tombs the bard doth rave,
You'll afk, how 'fcap'd he from the ftorm?
   What power hath fnatch'd him from the grave?
The Mufe the fecret will impart;
   (For what avails it to difguife?)
A fpeck he faw in Daphne's heart,
   That dimm'd the luftre of her eyes.
But, had the maid thy power poffefs'd,
   To bind and ftrengthen Beauty's charm;
The virtues glowing in thy breaft:
   The graces breathing in thy form:
Of manners gentle, and fincere,
   Had Daphne been what ——— is,
And had Misfortune's ftroke fevere
   Then robb'd him of his promis'd blifs,
Too big for words, the deep diftrefs
   Had quickly ftopp'd the Poet's tongue:
O'er-borne by Paffion's wild excefs,
   His heart had funk, unwept, unfung.

The

The youth, too fure, had " died unknown ;"
   No lover's figh his fhade had blefs'd ;
No rude memorial on his ftone
   Had mark'd his afhes from the reft ;
Unlefs, perchance, with one kind tear,
   The pitying maid his fate fhould mourn,
And bid fome happier fervant's care
   To throw a laurel on his urn.

A PASTORAL BALLAD, COMPOSED ONE HUNDRED
YEARS AGO.

GOOD-NATURE and Courtefy, fifters I ween,
   Twin daughters of Virtue the mother ;
In features fo like, that when fingle they're feen,
   Folks often take one for the other :
In gentle complacency, gefture, and grace,
   A difference fcarce could you fee ;
Save one, when you fpoke to her, fmil'd in your face;
   T'other modeftly bended the knee.

One fine Summer's morning refolved on a roam,
   They rofe with the lark, and as gay,
For as they intended to go far from home,
   They drefs'd themfelves out for the day :

                       Their

Their buſkin's they lac'd ſo to leave the knee bare,
  And move with a grace unconfin'd;
Their robes that were wont to flow looſe in the air,
  Were careleſsly tuck'd up behind,

Enſhrin'd in a ſcarf of a roſe colour'd hue,
  As ſplendid and bright as the morn!
A preſent which Hebe, the fair goddeſs, threw
  O'er their faces the day they were born:
While fragrance by Zephyr was pilfer'd away,
  And wafted all over the dale;
Their fair auburn treſſes a-looſe in diſplay,
  Were wantonly kiſs'd by the gale.

Thus array'd for the journey, and each to her mind,
  They chearfully walk'd on together;
Their ſteps were ſo light, left no traces behind,
  And their hearts were as light as a feather:
" Far weſtward," ſays Courteſy, " lives a fam'd knight,
  " Near a town in the mountains of Kerry;
" If fatigu'd, we'll repoſe at that ſeat of delight,
  " He was wont to be courteous and merry.

" Erſt often times happy we've ſung, danc'd and
      " play'd,
  " And frolick'd away with each other;
" Hand in hand o'er the lawn and the vallies we
    " ſtray'd,
  " They took us for ſiſter and brother:
                                        " Fame

" Fame fays, he's much chang'd fince he took a fair
  " bride,
 " Who prefides at the caftle of Dingle;"
" He fure won't forget us, Good-nature replied,
 " Who carefs'd us fo often when fingle."

Thus in chatting along they beguil'd away reft,
 Till at length they difcover'd a town;
Juft as Sol funk reclin'd upon Thetis's breaft,
 And Eve became dufky and brown;
When the caftle they fought for arofe in full view,
 Both their eyes and their hearts to delight;
Whofe fplendid appearance they very well knew,
 And its bountiful owner, the knight.

As they drew near the gate, they adjufted each grace,
 Which had fuffer'd, thro' toil and the weather,
The hair, the rude wind had blown over the face,
 They comb'd in, and tied up together;
Then rapt at the door, and each fent in her name,
 Which announc'd that two Ladies did wait;
Old acquaintance, they faid, and they thought it no
   fhame
 To pay him a vifit, though late.

When a dowdy-like figure, in riding attire,
 With as little of beauty as grace;
The cheeks all empurpl'd with fpots red as fire,
 Suffufing it o'er the whole face :

With

With arms fet a kimbo, and mafculine air,
　　Advanc'd like the caftle's defender;
Tho' the fex none can vouch, as it breeches did wear,
　　And feem'd of the *Epicene* gender.

But a fhrill female voice foon the woman declar'd,
　　Which pierc'd like the wind in December;
Affailing the ears of the Nymphs (who were fcar'd)
　　In words they have caufe to remember:
" How have ye the confidence, hulfeys," fhe cries,
　　" At this time of the night to alarm me?
" The names you fent in are a parcel of lies;
　　" You are *trulls* that belong to the army.

" The perfon you've had the affurance to name,
　　" Whofe former acquaintance you boaft;
" Its the worth of his ears to acknowledge your claim,
　　" While I'm at the *bead of the roaft*:
" Such *trollops* fhall never come near his domain,—
　　" So march off, and feek for new places;"
Then turn'd on her heel with an air of difdain,
　　And flapt the door full in their faces.

THE LAWYER's PRAYER.

A FRAGMENT.

BY DR. BLACKSTONE.

ORDAIN'D to tread the thorny ground,
Where few, I fear, are found ;
Mine be the confcience void of blame ;
The upright heart ; the fpotlefs name ;
The tribute of the widow's pray'r ;
The righted orphan's grateful tear !
To Virtue, and her friends, a friend ;
Still may my voice the weak defend !
Ne'er may my proftituted tongue
Protect th' oppreffor in his wrong ;
Nor wreft the fpirit of the laws,
To fanctify the villain's caufe !
Let others, with unfparing hand,
Scatter their poifon through the land ;
Inflame diffention, kindle ftrife ;
And ftrew with ills the path of life ;
On fuch, her gifts let Fortune fhower,
Add wealth to wealth, and power to power ;
On me, may favouring Heaven beftow,
That peace which good men only know.

The

The joy of joys, by few poſſeſs'd,
The eternal ſunſhine of the breaſt!
Power, fame, and riches, I reſign—
The praiſe of honeſty be mine;
That friends may weep, the worthy ſigh;
And poor men bleſs me when I die!

LOVE ELEGY. TO DAMON.

No longer hope, fond youth, to hide thy pain *,
  No longer bluſh the ſecret to impart;
Too well I know what broken murmurs mean,
  And ſighs that burſt, half-ſtifled, from the heart.

Nor did I learn this ſkill by Ovid's rule;
  The magic arts are to thy friend unknown:
I never ſtudied but in Myra's ſchool,
  And only judge thy paſſion by my own.

Believe me, † Love is jealous of his power;
  Confeſs by times the influence of the God;
The ſtubborn feel new torments every hour:
  To merit mercy, we muſt kiſs the rod.

* Non ego celari poſſim, quid nutus amantis,
    Quidve ferant miti lenia verba ſono
  Nec mihi ſunt fortes.———————   TIBUL.

† Deſine diſſimulare; Deus crudelius urit,
    Quos videt invitos ſuccubuiſſe ſibi.   TIBUL.

In

In vain, alas! you feek the lonely grove,
 And in fad numbers to the Thames complain:
The fhade, with kindred foftnefs, foothes thy love;
 Sad numbers foothe, but cannot cure thy pain.

When Phœbus felt (as ftory fings) the fmart,
 By the coy beauties of his Daphne fir'd,
* Not Phœbus felf could profit by his art,
 Though all the Nine the facred lay infpir'd.

Even fhould the maid vouchfafe to hear thy fong,
 No tender feelings would its forrows raife;
For, Verfe hath mourn'd imagin'd woes fo long,
 She'll hear unmov'd, and without pitying praife.

Nor yet, proud maid, fhould'ft thou refufe thine ear;
 Nor are the manners of the Poet rude;
Nor pours he not the fympathetic tear,
 His heart by anguifh, not his own, fubdu'd.

When faireft names in long Oblivion rot,
 (For faireft names muft yield to wafting Time)
The Poet's miftrefs 'fcape's the common lot,
 And blooms uninjur'd in his living rhime.

---

* Nec profunt Domino, quæ profunt omnibus artes. OVID.

IMITATION

IMITATION OF THE EIGHTH ODE IN THE THIRD
BOOK OF HORACE.

BY MR. HARRIS.

TO THE HON. THOMAS WINNINGTON, ESQ.

YOU aſk why bachelors take ſtate;
My little room, my ſcanty plate,
   Thus furbiſh'd out for dinner—
Eloquent Senator, this treat
Was vow'd when in wine-licence ſeat,
   You plac'd a half-ſtarv'd ſinner.

This day revolving, ſhall produce
My well-wax'd, choiceſt, ſacred juice
   Of Claret and Champagne,
Old Cyprus labell'd from renown,
Of battle fought, or taken town,
   In godlike Naſſau's reign.

O Winnington! now freely quaff,
Prolongs the revels and the laugh,
   Let Strife and Envy vaniſh;
Forget the ſtate and civil cares,
The realms of Auſtria rent in ſhares,
   Each German conteſt baniſh.

Spain

Spain shall submit, that slow tam'd foe,
France quits the meditated blow,
   Her samish'd fleet retiring ;
Soon Russia's sons shall fill the plain,
The balance England hold again,
   Walpole and George inspiring.

Of great affairs now wash your hands,
And leave the empty house to Sandys,
   Of business ever thinking ;
Let him and Gyb——n finish now,
The nothing that there's left to do,
   While we sit gaily drinking.

Forget for once all public cares,
All parli'mentary affairs,
   All precedents and order ;
Not e'en about elections think,
Nor sigh at the expence of drink,
   Dear glorious recorder.

But tell, when first by Polly mov'd,
How great your flame, how much you lov'd,
   How many times you kiss'd her—
Poor girl, deserted and forlorn !
This for the night—then in the morn,
   Fly with relays to Worcester.

ON CERTAIN NEW BUILDINGS NEAR THE ROYAL EXCHANGE.

WHEN Ifrael's impious fons forgot
The God, who their deliv'rance wrought,
   And fell before a calf of gold ;
Or when they fham'd the facred ufe
And worfhip of Jehovah's houfe,
   Build tables there, and bought and fold :

To ours, theirs were but puny crimes,
The Chriftian Jews of modern times
   Outdo the deeds of all their race :
They boldly tumble temples down,
And then, th' impiety to crown,
   Set up their idol in the place.

THE MIRROR OF KNIGHTHOOD.

A TRUE TALE WRITTEN IN THE YEAR 1734.

RIBBONS and ftars, and courtly toys,
Attract the wond'ring vulgar's eyes,
Who an implicit homage pay
To ev'ry thing that's glitt'ring gay ;

                           A dunce

A dunce, or what's inanimate,
A golden afs, or coach of ftate ;
But the difcerning few, the wife,
Truft not entirely to their eyes ;
For they confider Honour's badges
Are not true Merit's conftant wages.
Examples in all lands abound,
Except our own, where few are found :
And therefore, to avoid reflection :
A foreign tale is my election.

An Englifh merchant *, who for trade
His refidence Oporto made,
Liv'd in a houfe of ftructure odd ;
One wing extending to the road,
Which made a nook where people ftood,
The fountains of a briny flood.
Sol here intenfely darts his beams,
And raifes fuffocating fteams.
Our merchant, who could not endure
The nuifance, ftudied for a cure.
Should he defire them to forbear ;
A fhow'ry fky as foon would hear :
For they but fmall regard would fhow
A foreigner, their church's foe.
This brought to mind their fuperftition ;
(A lucky thought in his condition)

* The late Sir Robert Godfchall.

　　　　With

With that he for a workman fends,
Bids him forthwith the corner cleanfe,
And in it then a *crofs* erect,
(Object of Catholics refpect)
'Tis ; done the paffengers no more
Infeft the corner as before ;
But kneeling there, the *crofs* adore.

    The King, foon after, hapt to dub
With knighthood, a notorious fcrub :
(Ye Britons take my ftory right
'Twas Portugal that own'd the knight)
So ill beftow'd a grace became
Of converfation general theme :
When at our Merchant's table one,
On the fame fubject thus began ;
  " I muft confefs, I'm at a lofs,
  " How the King came to give the crofs
  " To fuch a wretch, the public fcorn !"
(The crofs their badge of knighthood worn)
Our Merchant, with a fmile, replies,
  " 'Tis done with reafon.   Kings are wife ;
  " The fame I've to my corner done,
  " That it might not be pifs'd upon."

THE CURSE OF AVARICE.

A SONG.

WHAT man in his wits had not rather be poor,
    Than for lucre his freedom to give ?
Ever bufy the means of his life to fecure,
    And fo ever neglecting to live.

Environ'd from morning till night in a croud,
    Not a moment unbent or alone ;
Conftrain'd to be abject, tho' never fo proud,
    And at every one's call but his own.

Still repining, and longing for quiet each hour,
    Yet ftudioufly flying it ftill ;
With the means of enjoying his wifh in his pow'r,
    But accurs'd in his wanting the will.

For a year muft be pafs'd ; or a day muft be come,
    Before he has leifure to reft ;
He muft add to his ftore this or that pretty fum,
    And then, will have time to be bleft.

But his gains, more bewitching the more they increafe,
    Only fwell the defires of his eye :
Such a wretch let mine enemy live, if he pleafe,
    Let not even mine enemy die.

H 2   EPIGRAM.

EPIGRAM.

A MISER ſpied a mouſe about his houſe;
What do you here, ſays he, my pretty mouſe?
Smiling, replies the mouſe, you need not ſweat,
I come for *lodging*, friend, and not for *meat*.

THE HONEST CONFESSION.

IT happen'd in a healthful year,
(Which made proviſions very dear
  And phyſic mighty cheap;)
A Doctor, ſore oppreſs'd with want,
On buſineſs turning out ſo ſcant,
  Was one day ſeen to weep.

A neighbour aſk'd him why ſo ſad,
And hop'd no dangerous illneſs had
  To any friend befel—
O Lord! you quite miſtake the caſe,
(Quoth Bliſter) Sir, this rueful face
  Is 'cauſe my friends are well.

THE

THE MORNING VISIT.

A DIALOGUE BETWEEN LADY RATTLE AND
LADY PAM.

L. R. GOOD morning, dear coufin, pray how do
you do ?
I hope you was fortunate laft night at loo.

L. P. No, truft me, I ne'er had fuch ill-luck before;
I loft a hundred fweet pieces, or more ;
The clock juft ftruck five as I went to bed,
Which caufes a fort of an ach in my head.
But prithee what news ?

L. R. ——Oh ! furprifing indeed !
Lord Razorface fain would perpetuate his breed,
And therefore he's married——

L. P. ——Heaven grant me repofe !
'Tis fome little wretch, fure, that nobody knows :
For no one of any diftinction would be
United to fuch a poor reptile as he.
His recent behaviour muft bar his purfuit ;
By all he's conjectur'd a fool or a brute ;
And befides he's no Lord, 'tis all a mere fiction,
Of that in the *cafe* we have thorough conviction.

H 3   L. R.

L. R. I have let you run on ; to enhance your
      furprife,
Take this paper, and fee ;—believe your own eyes.

L. P. Is't poffible ? No. Let me read it again ;
Such folly, fure, never infected a brain !
The am'rous Lady was at her laft pray'rs
To wed an impoftor— I'd wait till white hairs
Had grizzled my pate o'er, ere I wou'd unite
With one whofe connections would fhame me outright.

L. R. The new-married couple laft Friday appear'd
At Ranelagh—Lord how the company fneer'd,
To fee his mock Lordfhip fupporting his bride ;
Who hung, with a languifhing air, by his fide.
I vow and proteft 'twas diverting to hear
How often fhe fondly repeated, My dear !
Her female companion, as puffer, oft cried,
Lord ! where's Lady Razorface, where is the bride ?
Did you fee Lady Razorface ? it was her care
To buz the new title about ev'ry where.

L. P. 'Twas farcical, truly ; but tell me my dear,
If Lady Fannilia, her rival, was there ?

L. R. She was ; and look'd charming ;———I
      cannot exprefs
The p'eafing effect of her innocent drefs.

                              But

But what is more wonderful ftill, you muft know,
A Lady that died, as he faid, long ago ;
The daughter of him that you know made a noife :
Lord blefs me ! what makes me forget ?—the great
      caufe !

L. P.   Is it A————y's ?

L. R. —Yes ! you have hit it—the fame—
She that very night, fure to Ranelagh came :
And Nature fo lavifh has been to the Fair,
You'd have fworn that an angel was habitant there
The bridegroom, in fpite of his ignorant boaft,
Seem'd really as tho' he perceived a ghoft ;
His colour grew wan—though 'tis nat'rally fo,
But he was, I belive, unprepar'd for the blow.
She met him—he turn'd but too foon in the round,
She darted a glance—brighter fenfe might confound ;
And then in a tone quite ironical, cried,
I, two years ago, of a confumption died.
But pray, don't I look very well for a fhade ?
The malady was in my purfe tho' difplay'd :
But now I'm recover'd, you fee I'm grown fat
And D-n-v-n there fhall experience that :
My coufin Dorinda and I will unite,
And fee if our forces won't conquer him quite.
Confounded, he quitted the place with his bride,
And Wh—l—r, with fond admiration was ey'd.

L. P. I thank you, my dear, for your news; but
      you'll stay
And dine here to-day, in a family way;
Then at night repair with us to Lady Bragg's route,
And circulate what we've been talking about.

PHILO.

TO THE EDITOR.

SIR,

DINING at Lady Ramble's the other day, it was
proposed, after dinner, by her Ladyship's sister, to
hear Miss, who is a fine girl of about eleven years of
age, concerning some points she had been instructed
in relative to her duty in life; which being agreed
to, her Ladyship desired Miss to stand up, and then
asked the questions, and received the answers following: and as they may be of service to other young
Ladies of Quality, I have transmitted them to you.

SOCRATISSA.

L. R. My dear! pray tell me what you was brought
      into the world for?
MISS. A husband.
L. R. O my dear! you should say to be admired.

AUNT.

AUNT. Well, I vow I think my niece has given a
better anfwer ; as fhe came to the point
directly, and brought the matter home at
once.

L. R. What is the duty of an hufband ?

MISS. To pleafe his wife.

L. R. What is the duty of a wife ?

MISS. To pleafe herfelf.

L. R. What are the principal objects on which a
fine lady fhould fix her attention ?

MISS. Drefs and admiration.

L. R. What is the chief ufe of a fine lady's eyes ?

MISS To ftare and ogle at the men.

L. R. What is the bufinefs of a fine lady ?

MISS. To play at cards, go to routs, balls, plays,
operas, &c. and carry on intrigues.

L. R. What is the religion of a fine lady ?

MISS. To pay her devotions at court, and make her
curt'fies in the drawing-room.

L. R. May a fine lady ever go to church ?

MISS. Very feldom ! and then fhe muft be fure to
fleep there, or talk very loud, and flander
fome of her acquaintance.

L. R. Which is the beft book in the world ?

MISS. Hoyle on Quadrille.

L. R. From whence come the politeft fafhions, and
the beft filks ?

MISS. From France.

H 5
L. R.

L. R. Who make the beſt ſervants?

MISS. The French.

L. R. Very well, my dear! you don't forget, I find.

AUNT. I vow my niece is very perfect in her education, and will make a fine accompliſhed
woman.

A MODERN GLOSSARY.

ANGEL. The name of a woman, commonly of a very bad one.

AUTHOR. A laughing ſtock. It means likewiſe a poor fellow; and in general an object of contempt.

BEAR. A country gentleman; or, indeed, any animal upon two legs that doth not make a handſome bow.

BEAUTY. The qualification with which women generally go into keeping.

BEAU. With the article A before it, means a great favourite of all women.

BRUTE. A word implying plain-dealing and ſinceri-ty; but more eſpecially applied to a philoſopher.

CAPTAIN.
COLONEL. { Any ſtick of wood with a head to it, and a piece of black ribband upon that head.

CREATURE,

CREATURE. A quality expreffion, of low contempt, properly confin'd only to the mouths of ladies who are right honourable.

CRITIC. Like *homo*, a name given to all the human race.

COXCOMB. A word of reproach, and yet at the fame time fignifying all that is moft commendable.

DAMNATION. A term appropriated to the Theatre: though fometimes more largely applied to all works of invention.

DEATH. The final end of man; as well as of the thinking part of the body, as of all the other parts.

DRESS. The principal accomplifhment of men and women.

DULLNESS. A word applied by all writers to the wit and humour of others.

EATING. A fcience.

FINE. An adjective of a very peculiar kind, deftroying, or, at leaft leffening the force of the fubftantive to which it is joined, as fine gentleman, fine lady, fine houfe, fine cloaths, fine tafte !—in all which, fine is to be underftood in a fenfe fomewhat fynonymous with ufelefs.

FOOL. A complex idea, compounded of poverty, honefty, piety, and fimplicity.

GALLANTRY. Fornication and adultery.

GREAT. Applied to a thing, fignifies bignefs: when to a man, often littlenefs, or meannefs.

GOOD

GOOD. A word of as many different fenfes as the Greek word 'Eχω, or as the Latin *Ago*; for which reafon it is but little ufed by the polite.

HAPPINESS. Grandeur.

HONOUR. Duelling.

HUMOUR. Scandalous lies, tumbling and dancing on a rope.

JUDGE. }
JUSTICE. } An old woman.

KNAVE. The name of four cards in every pack.

KNOWLEDGE. In general, means knowledge of the town; as this is, indeed, the only kind of knowledge ever fpoken of in the polite world.

LEARNING. Pedantry.

LOVE. A word properly applied to our delight, in particular kinds of food; fometimes metaphorically fpoken of the favourite objects of all our *appetites*.

MARRIAGE. A kind of traffic carried on between the two fexes, in which both are conftantly endeavouring to cheat each other, and both are commonly lofers in the end.

MISCHIEF. Fun, fport, or paftime.

MODESTY. Aukwardnefs, rufticity.

NO-BODY. All the people in Great-Britain, except about 1200.

NONSENSE. Philofophy, efpecially the philofophical writings of the ancients, and more efpecially of Ariftotle.

OPPORTUNITY.

OPPORTUNITY. The feafon of cuckoldom.

PATRIOT A candidate for a place at court.

POLITICS. The art of getting fuch a place.

PROMISE. Nothing.

RELIGION. A word of no meaning; but which ferves as a bugbear to frighten children with.

RICHES. The only thing upon earth that is really defireable, or valuable.

ROGUE. ⎫
RASCAL. ⎭ A man of different party from your-felf.

SERMON A fleepy dofe.

SUNDAY. The beft time for playing at cards.

SHOCKING. An epithet which fine ladies apply to almoft any thing. It is, indeed, an interjection (if I may fo call it) of delieacy.

TEMPERANCE. Want of fpirit.

TASTE. The prefent whim of the town, whatever it be.

TEASING. Advice; chiefly that of a hufband.

VIRTUE. ⎫
VICE. ⎭ Subjects of difcourfe.

WIT. Prophanenefs, indecency, immorality, fcur-rility, mimickry, buffoonery; abufe of all good men, and efpecially of the clergy.

WORTH. Power, rank, wealth.

WISDOM. The art of acquiring all three.

WORLD. Your own acquaintance.

STANZAS

STANZAS TO THE LADIES.

ON THEIR HEAD-DRESS FOR THE YEAR 1768.

Tot premit ordinibus, tot adhuc compagibus altum
Ædificat caput; Andromachen a fronte videbis,
Post minor est, aliam credas.

HAVE ye never seen a net
  Hanging at your kitchen door,
Stuff'd with dirty straw, beset
  With old skewers o'er and o'er?

If you have—it wonder breeds
  Ye from hence should steal a fashion,
And should heap your lovely heads
  Such a deal of filthy trash on.

True, your tresses wreath'd with art
  (Bards have said it ten times o'er)
Form a net to catch the heart
  Of the most unfeeling lover.

But thus robb'd of half your beauty,
  Whom can you induce so high?
Or incline for love or suit t' ye
  By his nose, or by his eye?

When

When he views (what scarce I'd credit
  Of a sex so sweet and clean,
But that from a wench I had it,
  Of all Abigails the queen·)

When he views your tresses thin,
  Tortur'd by some French friseur,
Horse-hair, hemp, and wool within,
  Garnish'd with a diamond skewer.

When he scents the mingled steam,
  Which your plaster'd heads are rich in,
Lard and meal, and clouted cream,
  Can he love a walking kitchen?

SQUOXAM.

A SONG FOR THE MALL.

A PARODY ON WHITEHEAD'S SONG FOR RANE-LAGH.

BY A LADY.

YE foplings and prigs, and ye *wou'd-be* smart
    things,
  Who move in wide Commerce's round,
Pray tell me, from whence this absurdity springs,
  All orders of rank to confound?

What

What means the bag-wig, and the soldier-like air,
  On the tradesman obsequious and meek?
Sure Sabbaths were meant for retirement and pray'r,
  To amend the past faults of the week.

The youth, to whom battles and dangers belong,
  May call a fierce look to his aid;
Lace, bluster, and oaths, and a sword an ell long,
  Are samples he gives of his trade:
But you, on whom London indulgently smiles,
  And whom *counters* should guard from all ills,
Should slily invade with Humility's wiles,
  Let *splendor* deter us from *bills*.

Old Gresham, whose statue adorns the Exchange,
  Displays the grave cit to our view,
And silently frowns at a conduct so strange,
  So remote from your int'rests and you:
Then learn from his gesture, grave, decent, and plain,
  To copy fair Prudence's rules;
For Frugality's garb will conceal your vast gain,
  And secure ye the plunder of fools.

The ease of a court, and the air of a camp,
  Are graces no cit can procure;
Monsieur Jourdain * still plods in the Spitalfields
      tramp,
  Nor can Hart † the grown aukwardness cure:

* Vide Moliere's Gentleman Citizen.
† A dancing master in the city.

Thus

Thus if, apes of the fashion, St. James's you croud,
  And prefs onwards, in fpite of all ftops,
The Mall you may *fill*, and be airy and loud,
  But, truft me, you'll ne'er *fill* your fhops.

ON THE TEMPLARS.

As by the Templars holds you go,
  The horfe and lamb difplay'd,
In emblematic figures fhew
  The merits of their trade.

The client may infer from thence,
  How juft is their profeffion ;
The lamb fets forth their innocence,
  The horfe their expedition.

O happy Britons, happy ifle !
  Let foreign nations fay,
Where you get Juftice without guile,
  And law without delay.

THE ANSWER.

DELUDED men, thefe holds forego,
    Nor truft fuch cunning elves;
Thefe artful emblems tend to fhew
    Their clients, not themfelves.

'Tis all a trick, thefe are all fhams,
    By which they mean to cheat you;
But have a care, for you're the lambs,
    And they the wolves that eat you.

Nor let the thoughts of no delay,
    To thefe their courts mifguide you;
'Tis you're the fhowy horfe, and they
    The jockyes that will ride you.

A DESCRIPTION OF LONDON.

HOUSES, churches, mixt together,
Streets unpleafant in all weather,
Prifons, palaces contiguous,
Gates, a bridge, the Thames irriguous.

Gaudy things enough to tempt ye,
Showy outfides, infides empty;

Bubbles,

Bubbles, trades, mechanic arts,
Coaches, wheelbarrows, and carts.

Warrants, bailiffs, bills unpaid,
Lords of laundresses afraid:
Rogues that nightly rob and shoot men,
Hangmen, aldermen, and footmen.

Lawyers, poets, priests, physicians,
Noble, simple, all conditions;
Worth, beneath a thread-bare cover,
Villainy, bedaub'd all over.

Women, black, red, fair, and grey,
Prudes, and such as never pray;
Handsome, ugly, noisy, still,
Some that will not—more that will.

Many a beau without a shilling,
Many a widow not unwilling;
Many a bargain, if you strike it,
This is London!—How d'ye like it?

DESCRIPTION OF DUBLIN.

MASS-HOUSES, churches, mixt together;
Streets unpleasant in all weather;

The

The church, the four courts, and hell contiguous;
Caſtle, College-green, and Cuſtom-houſe gibbous.

Few things here are to tempt ye,
Tawdry outſides, pockets empty;
Five theatres, little trade, and jobbing arts,
Brandy, and ſnuff-ſhops, poſt-chaiſes, and carts.

Warrants, bailiffs, bills unpaid,
Maſters of their ſervants afraid;
Rogues that daily rob and cut men,
Patriots, gameſters, and footmen.

Lawyers, revenue-officers, prieſts, phyſicians,
Beggars of all ranks, age, and conditions;
Worth ſcarce ſhows itſelf upon the ground,
Villainy both with applauſe and profit crown'd.

Women lazy, dirty, drunken, looſe,
Men in labour ſlow, of wine profuſe;
Many a ſcheme that the public muſt rue it:
This is Dublin—if ye knew it.

A SKETCH OF PARIS.

LADIES, whoſe dreſs, wit, ſprightlineſs, and air,
Charm, till their plaiſter'd cheeks like ſpectres ſcare;

Men,

Men, learn'd, polite, and yet fo much the prig, |
Their genius feems quite center'd in their wig;
Ferries and ferrymen, begrim'd like Charon;
Plump, chuckling priefts, dreft gorgeoufly as Aaron;
Pulpit enthufiafts, foaming like mad Tom;
Coarfe vixins, ogling lewd in Notre Dame;
Pert, fallow, flipt-fhoed damfels, loofely drefs'd,
As rifen from bed, and panting to be prefs'd;
Shades, which the gazer for Elyfium takes,
'Till his ftung nofe fufpects the neighb'ring jakes;
Nuns, joking now, now fighing, " Flefh is grafs;"
Friars, who catches roar, and toaft a lafs;
An opera-houfe, large as our city halls,
Fine action, words, fcenes, dreffes—difmal fqualls!
Round from Pont-Neuf the view fuperb and rich;
Grand keys; the river a genteel Fleet-ditch;
Lame hackney horfes, as their drivers lean;
Figures unnumber'd, anti's to the fpleen;
Old wither'd cronies, in gaudy filks difplay'd;
Monks with toupees, and tonfors in brocade;
Tawdry, patch'd fempftreffes, befmear'd with fnuff;
Long-rapier'd pigmies, hid behind a muff;
Shoe-boys with ruffles; lacqueys drefs'd like qual—;
Such oddities! the town feems all a droll:
Turn where we will, our eyes new fplendors greet,
Whilft half the city glares a Monmouth ftreet.
Still motlier, Vanity, had been thy fair,
If the fam'd painter, Bunyan, had been there.

THE

THE BACHELOR's CHOICE OF A WIFE.

IF e'er I wed, my wife fhall not be old,
Deform'd, nor ugly, handfome, nor a fcold ;
She fhan't be pale, nor red, nor fhall fhe paint ;
Shall be religious too, but not a faint ;
She fhall have fenfe ; if not a wit, I'll take her :
Give fuch a wife, ye Gods, I'll ne'er forfake her.

THE FEMALE COMPLAINT.

BY A LADY.

CUSTOM, alas ! does partial prove,
   Nor gives us even meafure ;
A pain it is to maids to love,
   But 'tis to men a pleafure.

They freely can their thoughts difclofe,
   But ours muft burft within ;
Tho' Nature eyes and tongues beftows,
   Yet Truth from us is Sin.

Men to new joys and conquefts fly,
   And yet no hazards run ;
Poor we are left, if we deny ;
   And, if we yield, undone.

                       Then

Then equal laws let Cuſtom find,
　　Nor thus the ſex oppreſs ;
More Freedom grant to woman kind,
　　Or give to mankind leſs.

ON A YOUNG LADY,

BY A WILFUL MISTAKE READING, "RUBIES,"
FOR " BUBBIES"

WHEN wiſe philoſopher's explain
　　How gravity attracts,
The weighty pow'r they ſtill maintain,
　　All in the centre acts.

Thus tho' of earth the ſmalleſt part
　　The heavy impulſe owns,
Poize but the middle point with art,
　　You balance all the zones.

Hence ſages, when of ſpheres they write,
　　At centers fix a letter,
And wiſely call the body by't :
　　Take A, or chuſe a better.

If

If then on things we fix a name,
    We borrow from the middle,
How Mira's reading's not to blame,
    No longer is a riddle.

For though, that white as hills of fnow
    A bubby is, moft true be,
Peep flily thro' the gaufe, 'twill fhew
    The middle is a ruby.

                     E. L.

MISS COURTNEY TO MISS ANNE CONOLLY, MAY, 1753.

THO' kind your words—how full of forrow!
" Adieu! dear Bell—we part to-morrow!"
Farewel! dear fifter of my youth,
Ally'd by honour, love, and truth;
Farewel our vifits, fports, and plays,
Sweet folace of our childifh days;
Farewel our walks to Park and Mall,
Our jaunts to concert, route, or ball;
Farewel our difh of fprightly chat,
Of—who faid this—and who did that;
Critiques on fciffars, needles, pins,
Fans, aigrettes, ribbands, capuchins,

                     A long

A long farewell ! Conolly flies
To diftant funs, and diff'rent fkies !

A mufe in tears moves flow and dull
How weak the head, the heart fo full ?
Slight forrows find an eafy vent,
And trifling cares are eloquent ;
Sad filence only can exprefs
The genuine pains of deep diftrefs ;
Yet I cou'd rave in darkened chamber,
On feas of milk, and fhips of amber,
Like frantic Belvidera, when is
Perform'd the tragedy of Venice
Preferv'd—Oh ! as I hope to marry
Cibber is parted from her Barry ;
This by the by, may ferve as news
To-morrow on your way t'amufe,
It caufes great, great fpeculation—
Part of the bufinefs of the nation.

But hang digreffions—to return ;
And muft I three long winters mourn ?
That tedious length fpun out and paft
We meet--but how improv'd your tafte ?
Your figure, manner, drefs, and wit,
With all things for a Lady fit ;
For, *entre nous*, my dear, our faces
Should be the leaft of all our graces ;

VOL. VI.   I   If

If nought but Beauty wings the dart,
We ſtrike the eye but miſs the heart;
But huſh, and till we meet again,
Pray keep this ſecret from the men:
Should the weak things this truth diſcover,
How few coquettes would keep a lover!
And yet, ſo plain (tho' blind you know)
Milton could ſee it years ago:
Thus has the bard our ſex attackt,
" Fair outward, inward leſs exaẟ."
But you a ſtrong exception ſtand,
With Wit and Beauty hand in hand,
Apart how weak! combin'd how ſtrong!
They'll ſweep whole ranks of hearts along;
Before ſuch pow'rs each foe will fly,
That *principal*, and this *ally*.
Lovers you then will ſlay in plenty,
Like Bobadil each day your twenty;
Then will you grow the topic common,
" How ſoon, (they'll ſay) ſhot up a woman!
" What eyes! what lips! how fine each feature!
" Fore gad!—a moſt delicious creature!"——
This from the beaux—Mean time each belle, in
Mere ſpite, my dear, at your excelling,
Stung to the heart and deviliſh jealous
Of homage paid by pretty fellows,
Shall flirt her fan, and toſs, and ſnuff,
And cry—" The thing is well enough——

" But

" But for my foul, to fay what's true t'ye,
" I can't find out where lies her beauty."
Mean time you fmile with fweet difdain,
Like Dian 'midft her meaner train.

    Thus my prophetic foul foreknows
What Time fhall more anon difclofe.
Swift move that time on rapid wing,
And news of dear Conolly bring:
Yet let not thofe who love complain,
If thus to part is killing pain,
'Tis ftill to make the blifs more dear,
When the fweet hour of meeting's near.
So ftreams are fever'd in their courfe
To join again with double force.

ON THE RUINS OF POMFRET CASTLE.

Fatal and ominous to noble Peers,
Within the guilty clofure of thy walls,
Richard the Second, here was hack'd to death;
And, for more flander to thy difmal feat,
We give to thee our guiltlefs blood to drink.

              Earl Rivers' fpeech in Shakefpeare's Richard
            the Third. Scene, Pomfret Caftle.

LOOK round this vaft and venerable place,
Whofe ruin'd pile yet fhines with awful grace,

                                Majeftic

Majeftic ftill 'midft all it's faded charms :
   See the wide wafte of all·confuming Age,
   The wreck of ruthlefs wars and hoftile rage,
And all the dire effects of more than civil arms.

   View favage Time with cankering tooth devour
   The folid fabric of yon mould'ring tower,
That now in undiftinguifh'd chaos lies :
   Where erft the noble Lacey's * Norman line
   Plann'd the wide work, and form'd the vaft defign,
And bid with Gothic grace the ftately ftructure rife.

   When lo ! on high the vaulted domes fufpend,
   On lofty columns the wide arches bend,
And maffive walls the vaft domain inclofe :
   In vain the hoftile Warrior's nervous art,
   With miffive force directs the barbed dart,
Or with gigantic ftrength the pondrous jav'lin throws.

   For many an age, the Lacey's noble race
   W th arts and arms adorn'd the fplendid place,

* The family of Lacey, Earls of Lincoln and Hereford, came
in with the Conqueror, and were the greateft fubjects of thofe days.

As

As Heroes triumph'd, or as Patriots shone :
 Till with the great Plantagenet's fair bride *,
 In nuptial dower these ancient honours glide,
The seat of future Kings, that grac'd the English
  throne.

 On yonder hill, as ancient annals tell,
 The holy Hero, and the Martyr fell,
Which still, great Lancaster, thy mem'ry bears † :
 There, 'midst the Saints enroll'd, with rites divine,
 The pious Pilgrim sought the sacred shrine,
And bath'd thy hallow'd tomb with sympathizing
  tears.

 With holy zeal, and patriot graces arm'd,
 With all the powers of conscious Virtue warm'd,
'Midst Death's sad scenes the pious Martyr smiles ;
 In vain, proud Mortimer the hoary sage
 Bleeds, the sad victim of thy brutal rage,
Lost by thy lawless love, and all a woman's wiles,

 Look there, where erst yon mould'ring turret stood,
 Whose moss-grown stones are ting'd with royal
  blood,

 * Blanche, the heiress of Lacey, married the Duke of Lancaster,
with whom came the honour of Pomfret.

 † Thomas Duke of Lancaster was beheaded on the hill, which
is now called St. Thomas's Hill, by the intrigues of Mortimer and
the Queen of Edward the Second, and was afterwards canonized.

         'Midst

'Midſt civil broils the hapleſs Richard bled *;
 There cruel Exton's dark, aſſaſſin dart,
 With bloody treaſon pierc'd the Monarch's heart,
And fix'd the tottering crown on haughty Henry's
    head.

 Here, vaulting Bolingbroke, thy feeble foe,
 Felt in each whiſpering breeze the fatal blow,
Or heard Death's herald in each guilty ſtone :
 Short is the date of captive Monarch's doom,
 'Twixt the dark priſon and the yawning tomb,
For bold Ambition bears no rival to the throne.

 See yonder tower, ſtill bluſh with crimſon ſtains
 That flow'd in plenteous ſtreams from noble veins,
Where Vaughan and Gray by Glouceſter's arts ex-
    pir'd ;
 Where Rivers † fell, and with his lateſt breath
 Theſe mournful manſions dignified in death,
With Patriot virtues warm'd, and dawning Science
    fir'd.

* Richard the Second was murdered in Pomfret Caſtle, by Sir
Piers Exton, by order of Bolingbroke, afterwards Henry the Fourth.

† Sir Thomas Vaughan, and Richard Lord Gray, half-brother
to the Queen of Edward the Fourth, with Woodville Lord Rivers,
own brother to the ſame Queen, were all beheaded here at the
ſame time, by the intrigues of the Duke of Glouceſter, afterwards
Richard the Third. Earl Rivers was the great patron of learning,
and introduced Caxton to Edward the Fourth, who firſt brought
printing into England. See *Walpole's Noble Authors.*

'Midſt

'Midft the wide flames that civil difcord fpread,
When by bafe arts the royal Martyr bled,
Still loyal Pomfret fpurn'd the tyrant's hate;
   Laft in thefe northern * climes that fcorn'd to pay
   A fervile homage to his lawlefs fway,
And in inglorious eafe furvive their monarch's fate.

Long, haughty Lambert, did thy veteran powers
With iron tempeft fhake thefe folid towers,
And round the walls the miffive murder fend :
   In vain, brave Morrice, did thy martial train
   With loyal zeal the hoftile fhocks fuftain,
And 'gainft Rebellion's fons thefe royal domes defend.

Hark ! the loud engines tear the trembling walls,
And from its bafe the maffive fabric falls,
And all at once thefe antient honours fade :
   This princely pile with all it's fplendid fpoils,
   Sinks 'midft the havock of inteftine broils,
In proftrate ruins loft and dark Oblivion laid.

* Pomfret Caftle was the laft fortrefs in the north of England that
furrendered to the Parliament's forces, after the murder of King Charles,
and was befieged and deftroyed by General Lambert.

         THE

THE SCOTS DEGREE.

IN Scotland once a King they had
  The firſt that there did reign,
Tho' no man ever knew his dad
  Yet Fergus was his name.

This muckle Monarch on a day,
  To ſhew his Scottiſh pride,
Did to his nobles proudly ſay,
  As they ſtood by his ſide:

" Ken ye the man, or King, quo' he,
  " So great or wiſe as I ?
" His wit and ſtrength I fain would ſee,
  " For I the world defy,"

His muckle Lairds ſtood in amaze,
  And durſt no anſwer make,
For fear his paſſion they ſhould raiſe,
  And he their craigs would break.

But one much wiſer than the reſt,
  Had heard Religion's fame,
Told him that he, at his requeſt,
  Would tell a Monarch's name.

At

At which the mighty Monarch rofe,
 All fire, like a true Scot,
Bid him the fecret then difclofe,
 Or he fhould go to pot.

His name, quoth he, Jehovah is,
 The King of kings is he,
The fountain of all happinefs,
 The fupreme Deity.

" De'il fau me, if e'er I heard
 " Of fike a King before,
" Or ever ken'd I fike a Laird,
 " By fea or on the fhore.

" Gang ye'ere ways, gud-man, to that fame King,
 " And let him underftand,
" That you from me this meffage bring,
 " And that its my command;

" You tell him, he acknowledge muft,
 " That I'm the greater Laird,
" Or I'll his cities lay in duft,
 " His people put to th' fward."

This wonder of the Scottifh Court
 Did for a while retire,
To ufe his harmlefs rural fport,
 And quench his Monarch's fire.

       Some

Some time he ftaid, then came to Court,
   And ken'd was by the King,
" Weel man, quo' he, did'ft reach the port ?
   " What meffage doft thou bring ?"

" Troth have I, Sir, and thus he fays,
   " This meffage he does fend
" If you will love, and truft always
   " In him, he'll be your friend."

" Do's he, gud troth ? then deel a' me,
   " If any Scotifh man
" From this day e'er his kingdom fee,
   " Or e'er invade his land."

Thus, by a wife decree at firft,
   The Scotfmen loft their Heaven,
But to employ them, (thus accurs'd)
   The itch to them was given.

ON THE MODERN PLAID-WEARERS.

WHAT do I fee ridiculoufly clad
Our Englifh beaux and belles in Highland plaid ?
The drefs of rebels ! by our laws forbid !
No matter—why fhould friends or foes be hid ?

By

By this diftinctive badge are traitors fhewn,
Sure as free mafons by their fignals known.
Come to the mufter, Perkin, take thy roll,
And of thy flaves in liv'ry fum the poll.

Yet fay, ye daftards, who in peaceful days
Look big, drink healths, and hope a traitor's praife,
In what dark corner did ye lurk, when late
To the laft crifis Edward pufh'd his fate?
Sculking behind the laws ye wifh'd to break,
Ye dar'd rifk nothing for your Prince's fake;
Tamely ye faw his promis'd fuccours fail,
And William's arms, like Aaron's rod, prevail.
True to no fide, ye bats * of human kind,
Defpis'd by both, for public fcorn defign'd,
Still by your drefs diftinguifh'd from the reft,
Be James's forrow and be George's jeft.

FURYALUS.

AN EPIGRAM.

SEE Natta's coach along the village runs,
Drawn by four fcrubs, purfued by thrice four duns:
Landfkips and arms adorn the gay machine,
Without all Vanity, all Vice within.

* See Æfop's Fables.

The

The mob the gaudy pageant ftrikes, they gaze,
And, * B——ll; thy wond'rous art profufely praife:
In diff'rent views thy merit I explore;
Thy *works* furprife me, but thy *faith* much more.

EPIGRAM

OCCASIONED BY A GENTLEMAN'S LOSING FRE-
QUENTLY TO LADY H——RR——N AT LOO.

WHAT tho' I hold of trumps a flufh,
  And boaft a friend in pam;
Yet I dare own without a blufh,
  That I the lofer am.

Nay more, this happens every day,
  And is each night renew'd;
For who with H——rr——n can *play*
  And fail of being *loo'd.*

* The maker's name.

WRITTEN.

WRITTEN EXTEMPORE BY A YOUNG GENTLE-
MAN, FROM A MORNING VIEW ON A MOUN-
TAIN IN THE SOUTH OF WALES.

I.

How awful the morning breaks over yon hill,
   Not a whisper is heard on the plain,
Save the murmuring sweetness of yonder clear rill,
   By the mountains re-echoed again.

II.

See Phœbus how rosy he opens the day;
   See his beams how they sport in the stream;
Observe how contented that hind takes his way,
   And tackles his beasts to the team.

III.

From his straw-cover'd cot, just rose for the day,
   See Contentment and Health in his face;
The smiles of those bantlings his labours repay,
   The effects of a wholesome embrace.

IV. What

IV.

What a crowd of sweet prattlers! how healthy they
       look!
  Yet their tann'd little buffs are all seen;
Observe how they wantonly paddle in the brook,
  And race till they dry on the green.

V.

Had I on the side of yon mountain a cot,
  With a moderate competence blest,
I'd take a good wife, thank Heaven, for my lot,
  And consider the world as a jest.

THE GRAND CATHOLICON:

BEING A GENUINE FAMILY RECEIPT.

WRITTEN IN 1753.

To form a Minister, the ingredients
Are, a head fruitful of expedients,
Each suited to the present minute,
(No harm if nothing else be in it:)
The mind, tho' much perplex'd and harass'd,
The count'nance must be unembarrass'd:
High promises for all occasions:
A set of treasons, plots, invasions:

                           Bullies,

Bullies, to ward off each difaster:
Much impudence to brave his mafter;
The talents of a treaty maker;
The fole difpofal of the Exchequer.
Of right aud wrong no real feeling;
Yet in the names of both much dealing.
In fhort, this man muft be a mixture
Of broker, fycophant, and trickfter;
Who well can pack his cards, and tell 'em,
And knows as much as Mr. Pelham.

ON A LATE INCIDENT.*

Jam fatis Terris Nivis atque dira
Grandinis mifit Pater.   HOR.

THREE eminent men of the Law
   Lately travell'd on Sunday together,
Thro' roads that were cover'd with fnow,
   Not regarding the day nor the weather;

---

* *Thefe lines were written on feeing the following articles in the public prints:*

York, Jan. 20, 1767. We hear they have a prodigious quantity of fnow upon the Wolds; and that on Sunday, the 11th inft. as three gentlemen, eminent in the profeffion of the Law, were travelling from Pocklington to Hugget, they all three ftuck faft in a fnow-drift together, from which they were extricated with great difficulty.

At

At length they got into a pit
  (How difmal the tale to be told!)
Where they and their horfes—*to wit,*
  Had like to have perifh'd with cold.

Tho' they often before, none can doubt,
  Had waded thro' thick and thro' thin,
Yet the more now they try'd to get out,
  The deeper, alas! they funk in.

O Fortune! now lend 'em thine aid,
  Or how can'ft thou anfwer thy charge?
Thou hadft Coke upon Littleton laid,
  And pull'd down the *Statutes at large.*

The goddefs was mov'd with their cries,
  And determin'd to fave all their lives;
Then quick to their fuccour fhe flies,
  To the joy of their clients and wives.

Ye Lawyers, remember their doom,
  And be warn'd at the fall of thefe men:
I hope you will never prefume
  To travel on Sundays on again.

G. W—L—Y

A MOTTO

A MOTTO FOR THE HON. CHARLES YORKE, AN
ORATOR OF THE LONG ROBE—SPERO MELIORA.

A Noble ambition this motto reveals,
It tells you—the Orator hopes for the feals!

THE SCHOOL OF RHETORIC.

NEAR *London Bridge* once ftood a gate,
  Belinus, gave it name,
Whence the green *Nereids* oyfters bring,
  A place of public fame.

Here *Eloquence* has fixt her feat,
  The nymphs here learn by heart,
In *mode* and *figure* ftill to fpeak
  By modern rules of Art.

To each fair *oratrefs* this fchool
   Its *rhet'ric* ftrong affords ;
They double and redouble tropes
   With finger, fift, and words.

Both *nerves*, and *ftrength*, and *flow of fpeech*,
   With beauties ever new,
Adorn the language of thefe Nymphs,
   Who give to all their *due*.

O happy feat of happy Nymphs !
   For many ages known :
To thee each *roftrum*'s forc'd to yield,
   Each *forum* in the town.

Let other *academies* boaft
   What *titles* elfe they pleafe :
Thou fhalt be call'd *the Gate of Tongues*,
   Of tongues that never ceafe.   (T. P.)

ON A GENTLEMAN WHO MISTOOK A KEPT MIS-
TRESS FOR A LADY OF FASHION.

SIX tedious months young Damon figh'd,
   In vain his am'rous tale :
He fu'd, implor'd, Chlo ftill denied,
   No efforts could prevail.

At length he tried the pow'r of gold—
   She foon to chide forgot ;
The fair one was no longer cold,
   But prov'd—*alas ! too hot.*

V E R S E S

ADDRESSED TO SOME LADIES OF HAMPSTEAD.

CONSTANT gamefters ! every day
Ev'ry night, employ'd at play,
Squand'ring wealth and time away ;
Never happy but at cards,
You fhall meet with juft rewards,
(For neglect of family,
Trufted to a fervant's eye,

                        And

And domeſtic bus'neſs, care
Of each valuable fair)
Bane of quiet, peace, and joy,
Every comfort you deſtroy,
Whilſt your thinking friends bemoan,
Waſte and riot left at home :
Childrens ruin, huſbands curſe,
Prelude to an empty purſe ;
No man leaves to ſuch a wife
More than bare ſupport for life :
Have recourſe to common ſenſe,
Reform, or take the conſequence.

ON THE RUN OF ROMEO AND JULIET.

WELL—what to night? ſays angry Ned,
    As up from bed he rouſes :
Romeo again!—and ſhakes his head,
    An! pox on both your houſes.

UPON

UPON ST. GEORGE FOR ENGLAND.

St. GEORGE, to save a maid, the dragon flew;
A pretty tale, if all that's said be true;
Some say there was no dragon; and 'tis said,
There was no George;—I wish there was a maid.

THE LOYAL PAIR.

AN EPIGRAM.

I'LL *list* for a soldier, says Robin to Sue,
    T' avoid your eternal disputes;
Aye, aye, cries the termagant, do, Robin, do,
    I'll *raise*, the mean while, fresh recruits.

R. J.

ON A PRINTING-HOUSE.

THE world's a printing house; our words, our
    thoughts,
    Our deeds, are characters of sev'ral sizes;
Each soul is a compos'tor; of whose faults
    The Levites are correctors; Heav'n revises;

Death

Death is the common prefs ; from whence being driv'n,
We're gather'd, sheet by sheet, and bound for
Heav'n.

THE DIAMOND.

A FABLE.

LONG on Golconda's shore a diamond lay
Neglected, rough, conceal'd in common clay ;
By every passenger despis'd and scorn'd,
The latent jewel thus in secret mourn'd ; —
" Why am I thus to sordid earth confin'd,
" Why scorn and trod upon by every hind ?
" Were these bright qualities, this glittering hue,
" And dazzling lustre, never meant for view ?
" Wrapt in eternal shade if I remain,
" These shining virtues were bestow'd in vain."
As thus the long-neglected gem display'd
Its worth and wrong, a skilful artist stray'd
By chance that way, and saw, with curious eye,
Tho' much obscur'd, th' unvalu'd treasure lie.
He ground with care, he polish'd it with art,
And call'd forth all its rays from every part ;
And now young Delia's neck ordain'd to grace,
It adds new charms to Beauty's fairest face.

The mind of man neglected and untaught,
Is this rough diamond in the mine unwrought ;
Till Education lend her art, unknown
The brighteft talents lie, a common ftone ;
By her fair hand when fafhion'd, the new mind
Rifes with luftre, polifh'd and refin'd.

THE FARMER.

O Happy he ! happieft of mortal men !
Who, far remov'd from Slav'ry as from Pride,
Fears no man's frown, nor cringing waits to catch
The gracious nothing of a great man's nod ;
Where the lac'd beggar buftles for a bribe,
The purchafe of his honour ; where deceit,
And fraud, and circumvention, dreft in fmiles,
Hold fhameful commerce, and beneath the mafk
Of Friendfhip and Sincerity betray.
Him, nor the ftately manfion's gilded pride,
Rich with whate'er the imitative arts,
Painting or Sculpture, yield to charm the eye ;
Nor fhining heaps of maffy plate, unwrought
With curious, coftly workmanfhip, allure.
Tempted nor with the pride nor pomp of Power,
Nor pageants of Ambition, nor the mines
Of grafping Av'rice, nor the poifon'd fweets

Of

Of pamper'd Luxury, he plants his foot
With firmnefs on his old paternal fields,
And ftands unfhaken.   There fweet profpects rife
Of meadows fmiling in their flow'ry pride,
Green hills and dales, and cottages embower'd,
The fcenes of Innocence and calm Delight.
There the wild melody of warbling birds,
And cool refrefhing groves, and murm'ring fprings,
Invite to facred thought, and lift the mind
From low purfuits, to meditate the God!

LUCIAN's GREEK EPIGRAM,

INSCRIBED ON A COLUMN ERECTED IN A PIECE OF LAND, THAT HAD BEEN OFTEN BOUGHT AND SOLD; IMITATED.

I Whom thou fee'ft begirt with towering oaks,
Was once the property of John o'Nokes;
On him Profperity no longer fmiles,
And now I feed the flocks of John o'Stiles.
My former mafter call'd me by his name,
My prefent owner fondly does the fame;
While I, alike unworthy of their cares,
Quick pafs to captors, purchafers, or heirs.
Let no one henceforth take me for his own,
For Fortune! Fortune! I am thine alone.

A DESCRIPTION

A DESCRIPTION OF SPRING IN LONDON.

NOW new-made filks the Mercers' windows fhows,
And his fpruce 'prentice wears his Sunday cloaths,
His annual fuit with niceft tafte renew'd,
The reigning cut and colour ftill purfu'd.
The barrow now, with oranges a fcore,
Driv'n by at once a gamefter and a whore,
No longer gulls the ftripling of his pence,
Who learns that Poverty is nurfe to Senfe.
Much-injur'd trader whom the law purfues,
The law which wink'd, and beckon'd to the Jews ;
Why fhould the beadle drive thee from the ftreet ?
To fell is always a pretence to cheat.
" Large ftewing-oyfters" in a deepening groan,
No more refounds, nor " muffels" fhriller tone :
Seven days to labour now is held no crime,
And Moll " new mackrel" fcreams in fermon-time.
In ruddy bunches raddifhes are fpread,
And Nan with choice-pickt fallads loads her head ;
Now in the fuperb window Chriftmas green,
The bays and holly are no longer feen,
But fprigs of garden-mint in phials grow,
And gather'd laylock perifh as they blow.
The truant fchool-boy now at eve we meet,
Fatigu'd and fweating thro' the crowded ftreet,

His shoes embrown'd at once with dust and clay,
With Black-thorn loaded, which he takes for May ;
Round his flapp'd hat in rings the cowslips twine,
Or in cleft osiers form a golden line.
On milk-pail rear'd, the borrow'd salvers glare,
Topp'd with a tanker'd, which two porters bear,
Reeking, they slowly toil o'er rugged stones,
And joyless beldames dance with aching bones :
More blithe the powder'd tye-wigg'd sons of soot
Trip to the shovel with a shoeless foot.
In gay Vauxhall now saunter beaux and belles,
And happier cits resort to Sadler's-wells.

ON HAPPINESS.

O Happiness, where's thy resort ?
Amidst the splendor of a court !
Or, dost thou more delight to dwell
With humble hermit in his cell,
In search of truth ? Or, dost thou rove
Thro' Plato's academic grove ?
Or else, with Epicurus gay,
Laugh at the farces mortals play ?
Or with the Graces, dost thou lead
The sportive dance along the mead ?

Or,

Or, in Bellona's bloody car,
Exult amidft the fcenes of War ?
No more I'll fearch, no more I'll mind thee,
Fair fugitive—I cannot find thee !

THE CONQUEROR AND THE OLD WOMAN.

A FABLE.

A Perfian Monarch, one of thofe
  Whofe great ambition knew no bound ;
Some Cyrus, or Darius, we'll fuppofe,
  In whom no other vice was found,
If we dare name ambition fo,
For fome doubt whether it be vice or no ;
I have not time at prefent to confute,
So grant the queftion, rather than difpute.
This Sophi far and wide his conquefts fpread ;
  Full thirty crowns, or more,
Were pil'd on his anointed head,
  And yet the weight with eafe he bore ;
For'twas his great and chief delight
  To break the yoke his vanquifh'd fubjects wore,
And make their burden light.
  Attentive to the voice of the diftrefs'd,
Juftice and Virtue flourifh'd in his reign ;
When from the confines of his vaft domain
  A good old woman who had been opprefs'd,

K 2   C am

Came to the footstool of his throne
　To have her grievances redress'd ;
And thus in piteous, tragic tone
　His Majesty addrefs'd :—
" Encourag'd by your fame, I come from far ;
" Sir, you're our King by right of War ;
" By right of fubject I for Juftice fue :
" I claim it, and you'll grant it ; 'tis my due.
" My daughter ravifh'd, and my houfe deftroy'd,
" And all by one whom you employ'd
" To act the King in place of you."
" I doubt not but all this is true,"
　The confcious Prince replied ;
" But fo far off what can I do ?
　" To make my people happy is my pride :
　" And yet I cannot every where refide.
" The Sun, which all the world furrounds,
" Shines and enlivens but to certain bounds ;
" The reft are dark and cold."
" That's argu'd ill, if I may be fo bold,"
　Return'd the matron to the Sovereign,
" 'Twas weak to grafp at what you cannot hold,
　" And conquer more than you can govern."
While o'er the fea of Life we take our trip,
　Kings are by Heav'n commiffion'd to command ;
Captains, not owners of the fhip,
　'Tis theirs to fteer the people fafe to land :

　　　　　　　　　　　　And

And when the bark with Prudence they convey,
We row with pleafure, and with pride obey.

THE ART OF COQUETRY.

BY MRS. CHARLOTE LENOX.

YE lovely maids whofe yet unpractis'd hearts
Ne'er felt the force of Love's refiftlefs darts ;
Who juftly fet a value on your charms,
Pow'r all your wifh, but beauty all your arms ;
Who o'er mankind would fain exert your fway,
And teach the lordly tyrant to obey :
Attend my rules to you alone addreft,
Deep let them fink in every female breaft.
The Queen of Love herfelf my bofom fires,
Affifts my numbers, and my thoughts infpires ;
Me fhe inftructed in each fecret art,
How to enflave, and keep each vanquifh'd heart ;
The figh that heaves by ftealth, the ftarting tear,
The melting languifh, the obliging fear,
Half-utter'd wifhes, broken, kind replies,
And all the filent eloquence of eyes ;
To teach the Fair by various wiles to move
The foften'd foul, and lead the heart to Love.
Proud of her charms, and confcious of her face,
The haughty beauty calls forth every grace,
With fierce defiance throws the killing dart ;
By force fhe wins, by force fhe keeps the heart.

The

The witty Fair a nobler game purſues,
Aims at the head, but the rapt ſoul ſubdues.
The languid Nymph enſlaves with ſofter art,
With ſweet neglect ſhe ſteals into the heart,
Slowly ſhe moves her ſwimming eyes around,
Conceals the ſhaft, but meditates the wound.
Her gentle languiſhments the gazers move,
Her voice is Muſic and her looks are Love :
To few tho' Nature may theſe gifts impart,
What ſhe withholds, the wiſe can win from Art.
Then let your airs be ſuited to her face,
Nor to a languiſh tack a ſprightly grace.
The ſhort round face, briſk eyes, and auburn hair,
Muſt ſmiling Joy in every motion wear,
The quick unſettled glance muſt deal around,
Hide all deſign, and ſeem by chance to wound :
Dark rolling eyes a languiſh may aſſume,
Theſe the ſoft looks and melting air become :
The penſive head upon the hand reclin'd,
As if ſome ſweet diſorder fill'd the mind ;
Let the heav'd breaſt a ſtruggling ſigh reſtrain,
And ſeem to ſtop the falling tear with pain.
The youth, who all the ſoft diſtreſs believes,
Soon wants the kind compaſſion that he gives ;
But Beauty, Wit, and Youth, may ſometimes fail,
Nor alway's o'er the ſtubborn ſoul prevail ;
Then let the fair-one have recourſe to Art ;
Who cannot ſtorm may undermine the heart.

First

First form your artful looks with studious care,
From mild to grave, from tender to severe ;
Oft on the careless youth your glances dart,
A tender meaning let each glance impart.
Whene'er he meets your looks with modest pride,
And soft confusion, turn your eyes aside ;
Let a soft sigh steal out, as if by chance,
Then cautious turn and steal another glance.
Caught by these arts, with Pride and Hope elate,
The destin'd victim rushes on his fate :
Pleas'd, his imagin'd victory pursues,
And the kind maid with soft attention views ;
Contemplates now her shape, her air, her face,
And thinks each feature wears an added grace ;
Till Gratitude, which first his bosom proves,
By slow degrees sublim'd, at length he loves.
'Tis harder still to fix than gain a heart ;
What's won by Beauty, must be kept by Art.
Too kind a treatment the blest lover cloys,
And oft Despair the growing flame destroys.
Sometimes with smiles receive him, sometimes tears,
And wisely balance both his hopes and fears.
Perhaps he mourns his ill-requited pains,
Condemns your sway, and strives to break his chains ;
Behaves as if he now your scorn defied,
And thinks, at least, he shall alarm your pride :
But with indifference view the seemed change,
And let your eyes to seek new conquests range ;

K 4   While

While his torn breaſt with jealous fury burns,
He hopes, deſpairs, adores, and hates by turns ;
With anguiſh now repents the weak deceit,
And powerful paſſion bears him to your feet.
Strive not the jealous lover to perplex,
Ill ſuits ſuſpicion with that haughty ſex ;
Raſhly they judge, and always think the worſt,
And Love is often baniſh'd by Diſtruſt :
To theſe an open free behaviour wear,
Awful diſguiſe, and ſeem at leaſt ſincere ;
Whene'er you meet, affect a glad ſurprize,
And give a melting ſoftneſs to your eyes :
By ſome unguarded word your love reveal,
And anxiouſly the riſing bluſh conceal.
By arts like theſe the jealous you deceive,
Then moſt deluded when they moſt believe.
But while in all you ſeek to raiſe deſire,
Beware the fatal paſſion you inſpire :
Each ſoft intruding wiſh in time reprove,
And guard againſt the ſweet invader—Love.
Not for the tender were theſe rules deſign'd,
Who in their faces ſhow their yielding mind :
Whoſe eyes a native languiſhment can wear,
Whoſe ſmiles are artleſs, and whoſe bluſh ſincere ;
But for the Nymph who liberty can prize,
And vindicate the triumph of her eyes :
Who o'er mankind a haughty rule maintains,
Whoſe Wit can manage what her Beauty gains :

Such

Such by thefe arts their empire may improve,
And, unfubdu'd, controul the world by Love

AN INSCRIPTION.

WRITTEN UPON ONE OF THE TUBS IN HAM
WALKS, SEPTEMBER, 1760.

DARK was the fky with many a cloud,
 The fearful lightnings flafh'd around,
Low to the the blaft the foreft bow'd,
 And bellowing thunders rock'd the ground.

Faft fell the rain upon my head,
 And weak and weary were my feet,
When lo ! this hofpitable fhed
 At length fupplied a kind retreat.

That in fair Memory's faithful page
 The Bard's efcape may flourifh long,
Yet fhuddering from the tempeft's rage,
 He dedicates the votive fong.

For ever facred be the earth
 From whence the tree its vigour drew !
The hour that gave the feedling birth !
 The foreft where the fcyon grew !

K 5

Long

Long honour'd may his afhes reft,
　　Who firft the tender fhoot did rear !
Bleft be his name !——but doubly bleft
　　The friendly hand that plac'd it here !

O ne'er may war, nor wind, nor wave,
　　This pleafurable fcene deform,
But Time ftill fpare the feat which gave
　　The Poet fhelter from the ftorm.

A SONG.

BY A NOBLE LORD.

RESOLV'D, as her Poet, of Cælia to fing,
For ideas of Beauty I fearch'd thro' the Spring;
To flowers foft blooming compar'd the fweet maid;
But flowers, tho' blooming, at ev'ning may fade.

Of fun-fhine and breezes I next thought to write,
Of the breezes fo foft, and the fun-fhine fo bright;
But thefe with my Fair no refemblance will hold,
For the fun fets at night, and the breezes grow cold.

The clouds of mild ev'ning array'd in pale blue,
While the fun-beams behind them peep glittering
　　　　through,
Tho' to rival her charms they can never arife,
　Yet, methought, they look'd fomething like Cælia's
　　fweet eyes.

　　　　　　　　　　　　　　　　　Thefe

These beauties are transient, but Cælia's will last,
When Spring, and when Summer, and Autumn are
   past ;
For sense and good humour no season disarms,
And the soul of my Cælia enlivens her charms.

At length, on a fruit-tree a blosom I found,
Which beauty display'd, and shed fragrance around,
I then thought the Muses had smil'd on my pray'r,
This blossom, I cried, will resemble my Fair !

These colours so gay, and united so well,
This delicate texture and ravishing smell,
Be her person's sweet emblem ! but where shall I find,
In Nature, a beauty that equals her mind !

This blossom so pleasing, at Summer's gay call,
Must languish at first, and must afterwards fall,
But behind it the fruit, its successor, shall rise,
By Nature disrob'd of its beauteous disguise.

So Cælia, when Youth, that gay blossom, is o'er,
By her virtues improv'd shall engage me the more,
Shall recall ev'ry beauty that brighten'd her prime,
When her merit is ripen'd by Love and by Time.

JOHN

JOHN, THE ENGLISH FOOTMAN.

A TALE.

THE chiming bells from ev'ry fteeple
Proclaim'd to well difpofed people,
That they muft be repairing foon
To fervice of the afternoon :
That is—it now was almoft three;
My Lord, ftill at his morning tea,
(For it was Sunday, and you know
What then good folks of fafhion do)
My Lady holds engag'd in chat,
In blaming this, reforming that :
" Since, my dear Lord, at your command,
" I took the management in hand,
" You know, 'twas always my endeavour,
" Your houfe fhould be polite and clever.
" How well your dignity it fuits
" To have difcharg'd your Englifh brutes !
" I think, there now remains but one—
" And he, becaufe your tenant's fon !
" Muft we be plagu'd with fuch a fot,
" In complaifance to Farmer Trot ?"
My Lord replies,— " Trot pays his rent,
" And can make votes to Parliament :
" And often fends us chines and turkies ;
" And John too, capable of work is."

" Send

" —Send him to work then in the ftable—

" Oh! fuch a wretch to wait at table!

" Indeed, my dear, it gives me pain,

" To fee him fhock the *Gens de bien*

" With toes turn'd in and aukward mien!

" So this I do infift upon,

" That he immediately be gone!"

" Since 'tis your pleafure, go he muft—

" Yet to affign fome caufe—were juft—

" At leaft what plaufible may feem—

" And that's confiftent with my fcheme.

" In the militia we will fwear him;

" I'll write to Fielding not to fpare him:

" Thefe purpofes will anfwer double,

" Firft, in difcharging you of trouble,

" And in procuring me the merit

" Of acting with a gen'rous fpirit:

" My Lord (they fay) don't even fpare

" His own domeftics from the war;

" How ardent for the public weal!

" Example rare of public zeal!

" But let us found him firft, to know

" Whether the rogue's inclin'd to go:

" If you, my dear, approve the meafure,"—

" Yes—call him up"—My Lord, your pleafure.

" John, thou'rt a fellow tall and lufty,

" Of heart right found, and courage trufty;

" Can

" Can you yourself in humour bring
" To serve your country and your King,
" And straight some Justice go before,
" In the militia to be swore ?"
Militia !——What is that, my Lord?
I do not understand the word——
" Why, John, it means the French (ah, hang 'em!)
" Soundly, whene'er you meet, to bang 'em"—
Is that the case ?—with all my heart—
I'll do my best to play my part—
John straight retires, with aukward airs;
And meets the valet on the stairs,
Whom he accosts with one salute
Of rightly pois'd, elastic foot,
Which sent Monsieur a headlong falling,
And left him at the bottom sprawling.
My Lord's friseur he next attacks
With frequent cuffs, and English thwacks;
And, while he dress'd my Lady's tête,
John curl'd his locks and comb'd his pate.
Then hurrying in the kitchen goes,
And bastes the cook and tweakes his nose ;
" Vat be de mater, villian, rogue,
" Me kill you, thou one English dog !"
Soho, quoth John, Monsieur Ragou,
Since you thus froth and splutter so,
I must apply my drudger too ;

If

If that won't do—you shall, unpitied,
Be sent to Garrick to be spitted.
Janton he nexts attacks, and throws
Over her head at once her cloaths :
(And sad disaster ! found— to shock one,
That poor Janton had no smock on !)
Who hurries strait to Ma'moiselle,
Enrag'd her loud complaints to tell ;
Who, interfering in the rout,
" Fine vark indeed dis, Maitre Trotte !
" I'll do your bus'nefs strait," she cries,
And up stairs to my Lady flies,
And scarce, quite out of breath, could say,
" *Eb ! quelles barbares, quelles sots Anglois !*
" Trot has been making such a riot ?"
The scoundrel Trot, Lord, Lady cry out—
Your valet—Cook—and Friseur bang'd :
——Send him to Fielding to be hang'd !
" And in the fight of the postilion
" O'er Janton's head cast her *cotillon* ;
" And *vat vas varse, à mon surprise,*
" *Pauvre Janton* had no *Chemise.*"
Go, hang him without Judge or Jury,
Cries out my Lady, in a fury.
John summon'd now before e'm all,
With aching heart attends the call.
" *Fripon, poltron,* vile English varlet,"
My Lady screams, as red as scarlet ;

While

While the soft voice of Ma'moiselle
With poll and lap-dog join the yell.
Poor John, confus'd with wild dismay,
Trembling, and fault'ring, scarce could say,
Only—one word—My Lord, I pray,
I'm sorry thus to have offended,
But I no harm at all intended.
Your Lordship's orders, and my oath,
You know, my Lord, oblige me both
To maul the French, to bang and beat 'em
In whatsoever place I meet 'em.
" Hold, John—you quite mistake the matter,
" But not on this side of the water;
" In Flanders beat 'em if you can;
" And there you'll shew yourself a man.
" Or if they ever should be found
" To land their force on British ground,
" Why then you might exert your sallies,
" To drive them back again to Calais.
" The French so ever *degagé*,
" So airy, gay, polite, and free,
" The object of the vulgar spite,
" By long prescription have a right
" To the protection of the great,
" Who live in affluence and state :
" Whom our domestics, when we stile 'em,
" Our houses are their sure asylum;

" Their

" Their characters are sacred there ;
" So that, if saucy scoundrels dare
" I ' insult their persons, or to bait 'em,
" 'Tis constru'd *Scandalum magnatum* ;
" Then breach of privilege ensues,
" With fines, imprisonments, and dues :
" Nor, till unto our wills we bend 'em,
" Can *Habeas Corpus's* defend 'em.
" Therefore, for your presumption, John,
" Uncase this moment—and be gone !"

THE LAUGHING PHILOSOPHER.

WHEN I take an attentive survey of mankind,
From their follies and vices diversion I find ;
Their humours, caprices, their whims and odd ways,
Sensations of mirth in me constantly raise.
Every place is with curious, choice characters stor'd,
Which, from morning to night, entertainment afford.
In each lane, in each alley, court, square, row, or
          street,
Scenes, truly Hogarthian, I fail not to meet ;
Scenes which would not in many a muscle provoke,
But I from the dullest can strike out a joke.
In every man's motions I merriment trace,
And can laughter extract from the dismallest face.

When

When I fee men and women induftrioufly fhun
Their own thoughts, and each ev'ning to card-tables
    run ;
When dowagers, drefs'd up like girls of fifteen,
In the front of a fide-box are mad to be feen ;
When a blooming young creature to threefcore is tied,
That to routs and to plays fhe in diamonds may ride ;
When Ladies, to fhew their no learning, talk Latin,
And Tradefmen their fcabbards adorn with white
    fatin ;
When a poor Tallow-chandler, deceas'd, lies in ftate,
Who alive, perhaps, had not five pounds worth of
    plate ;
When fat-headed Aldermen fet up for wit,
With laughter my'fides are juft ready to fplit :
When a pert Temple beau the fine gentleman apes,
And 'prentices brag of their duels and rapes ;
When a young academic afcends, with an air,
To the pulpit, and tries to attract all the Fair,
And oft, in the midft of his flow'ry difcourfe,
Looks around to obferve if his eyes have had force ;
When travell'd young fops talk of nothing but France,
When old maids learn to fing, and grown gentlemen
    dance ;
When pious Ned Shuter at Whitfield's appears,
I laugh till my eyes are bedim'd with my tears.
When women neglect their domeftic,affairs,
And puzzle their heads with political cares ;
                 When

When with zeal patriotic they puddings defpife,
And chatter of taxes, and loans, and fupplies;
When thofe who have nothing to lofe fume and fret
At the lownefs of ftocks and the national debt,
And rail at the court in a paffionate ftile,
I hollow fo loud, you may hear me a mile.

A DIALOGUE

BETWEEN A GENTLEMAN AND A PAINTER AT THE EXHIBITION IN SPRING-GARDENS, IN THE SPRING, 1770

GENT.

MR. Painter, you joke
With us peaceable folk,
For furely it never can be
    That three brave fons of Mars,
    Can be talking of wars,
Whilft, like miffes, they're fipping their tea.

PAINT.

Thefe are foldiers indeed,
But their trade's not to bleed,

'Tis

'Tis true, they wear long fwords and boots ;
   Yet they deem it no fin
   To fleep in whole fkin,
So ne'er venture to ftain e'en their coats.

   Should I paint them in arms,
   'Midft hoftile alarms,
What mortals a fmile could refufe ?
   For tho' daggers they fpeak,
   Were their country at ftake,
Yet, like Hamlet, Sir, none would they ufe.

   'Tis theirs in the Mall
   To attract the foft belle,
Who every day haunts the Parade ;
   For the fair love the brave,
   And ftill firmly believe
They muft be fo who wear a cockade.

GENT.

   I allow your remark,
   But 'tis not in the Park,
That their prowefs have vanquifh'd the fair ;
   There is no one but knows
   How they flaughter'd their foes
In the battle of Bloomfbury-fquare.

PAINT.

PAINT.

When Ulyſſes, ſcot free,
'Scap'd the ſword and the ſea,
As Ovid relateth the fable;
He deſcrib'd to his wife,
Where he ventur'd his life,
By the wine he had ſpilt on the table.

Juſt ſo theſe repoſe,
After routing their foes,
In that bluſt'ring, bloodleſs campaign;
So now, Sir, you ſee,
With what's ſpilt of their tea,
They are fighting it over again.

" Here the troopers I led
" When the enemy fled,
" And there, Sirs, I loſt my new beaver;
" Here a Taylor's aſſault
" Caus'd the firſt line to halt,
" And there I encounter'd a Weaver."

BOBADIL.

PRESENT PUBLIC WISHES.

THE K— *wiſhes* to be *quiet*.
The people *wiſh* him to be *great*,

The

The Miniſtry *wiſh* to continue the majority.

Patriots *wiſh* for Liberty.

Remonſtrants *wiſh* for redreſs.

Old maids *wiſh* for young huſbands.

Many huſbands *wiſh* for divorces.

The proprietors of Ranelagh and Vauxhall *wiſh* for
    fair weather.

Chairmen *wiſh* for foul weather.

Convicts *wiſh* for life.

Wilkes *wiſhes* no longer for his liberty.

His creditors *wiſh* him joy of it.

The *outs* *wiſh* to be *in*.

The *inns* *wiſh* to continue ſo.

Sore conſciences *wiſh* for a reſtriction on the preſs.

Players *wiſh* for good benefits.

Vagabonds *wiſh* for a revolution

In every branch of the conſtitution.

And the writer of this rhapſody *wiſhes* he had clear,

No more, nor leſs, than juſt one thouſand pounds a
    year.

EPISTLE FROM LADY BRIDGET LANE, TO LADY
BAB BUTTERFLY, AT YORK.

BY CAPTAIN THOMSON.

YOU cannot imagine, my dear Lady Bab,
How anxious I am all my budget to blab;

                  But,

But, Lord, I could tell you a thousand times better,
Than scribbling my thoughts, like a clerk, in a letter:
But when we're apart, there is no other means
Of describing the vulgar, and St. James's scenes—
Well, then to begin, my dear Bab, and be short;
In the presence I was, when the May'r came to court;
Ye Gods! what a shame! that the scum of the earth
Should dare to petition as people of birth:
Such a fight, my dear Bab, with their gowns and
    broad faces,
With their vile vulgar gaits, and their staves and
    their maces;
But, like owls in the Sun, how our King made them
    blink!
And then, my dear soul, how these creatures did stink!
I declare *eau de luce* hardly kept me from fainting;
A plague e'en in Turkey, was not half so tainting:
But the King, my dear child, who is alway so clear,
Sent the wretches away with a flea in their ear.
You know how I sigh'd for a prize in the Lottery;
But now all my sighs are turn'd round on the Coterie:
Between you and me, I'd lay twenty to seven,
That many had rather go there than to Heaven;
Its the snuggeft affair, and the pleasantest plan,
For altho' with your husband—you may have a man;
Do you know tho', they've black-ball'd George Sel-
    wyn and March;
(That sweet Macaroni, so stiff and so starch)
          Their

Their reafons I know not ; but fure it is cruel,
For of all our gay Lords, fure my Lord is the jewel;
As for Selwyn, the creature has wit and good fenfe,
Which to me, Lady Bab, is a horrid offence.
What you lofe my dear creature, by not being in town!
Foote's open, and Reynolds's paintings are fhewn :
Enchanting Vauxhall, where the dark-walls fo fnug,
Afford me, at times, a dear kifs, and a hug.
Well, adieu, Lady Bab, for engagements are preffing ;
I dine at Almack's—and have not began dreffing ;
To reach the dear fpot, I am all in a fidget,
And beg to remain, Bab—your dear little

BRIDGET.

IN THE SEASON OF 1760.

THE SUBSCRIPTION-BOOKS AT BATH WERE OPENED
FOR PRAYERS AT THE ABBEY, AND GAMING AT THE
ROOMS.
IN THE EVENING OF THE FIRST DAY THE NUMBERS STOOD
AS UNDER.

THE Church and Rooms the other day,
Open'd their books for Pray'r and Play ;
The Prieft got twelve—Hoyle fixty-feven ;
How great the odds for Hell 'gainft Heaven !

AN

AN ANSWER.

IF figning with the twelve, to Heaven
   The fureft way does fhew,
And figning with the fixty-feven,
   As fure to Hell to go:

Tim, prithee fay, thou knowing elf,
   (For to decide I'm loth)
Where go the reft, who with thyfelf,
   Perhaps have fign'd with both?

Thus Juftice fays, at her court leet,
   (And Juftice is no ftinter)
" In Heav'n you'll have a Summer feat,
   " In Hell a houfe for Winter."

EPIGRAM.

SAYS Ch—dl—gh to a certain dame,
   Whom royal horners woo,
I almoft think it is a fhame
   To talk to fuch as you.

We both, replied the titled whore,
    Have been a theme for laughter;
The diff'rence this, *you* felt before,
    My foible happen'd after.

ON A BLACK MARBLE STATUE OF A SLAVE STANDING IN ONE OF THE INNS OF COURT.

IN vain, poor fable fon of woe,
    Thou feek'ft a tender ear;
In vain thy tears with anguifh flow,
    For Mercy dwells not here.

From Cannibals thou fly'ft in vain:
    Lawyers lefs quarter give;
The firft won't eat you till you're flain,
    The laft will do't alive.

ON SEEING A LAW-BOOK

BOUND IN UNCOLOURED CALF, AND WHITE EDGES.

WITH unftain'd edges, and in fpotlefs calf,
A Law-book bound muft make a ftoic laugh;
                    For

For in that ftriking emblem you may fee,
Not what the Law *is*, but what the Law *fhould* be :
A Law-book thus in the Law Livery dreft,
Is like a Jefuit in a Layman's veft ;
'Tis like a ftrumpet cloath'd in fpotlefs white ;
'Tis like a bitter apple, fair to fight ;
'Tis like a fimple Quaker, plain and neat,
That with his yeas and noes is fure to cheat ;
'Tis like a pirate, that falfe colours fhows,
Or Hecla's flames conceal'd in virgin fnows ;
'Tis like—in fhort, 'Tis like Dan Milton's fin ;
All fair without, but monftrous foul within.

WRITTEN UNDER A PICTURE OF KITTY FISHER.

DRAWN IN THE CHARACTER OF CLEOPATRA.

To this fam'd character how juft thy right !
Thy mind as wanton, and thy form as bright.

A BALLAD,

A BALLAD, BY THE EARLS OF CHESTERFIELD AND BATH.

[See Swift's Works, vol. xviii. p. 324.]

I.

THE Mufes quite jaded with rhyming,
   To Molly Mogg bid a farewel,
But renew their fweet melody chyming,
   To the name of dear Molly Lapel.

II.

Bright Venus yet never faw bedded,
   So perfect a beau and a belle,
As when Hervey the handfome was wedded
   To the beautiful Molly La—l.

III.

So powerful her charms, and fo moving,
   They would warm an old Monk in his cell,
Should the Pope himfelf ever go roving,
   He would follow dear Molly La—l.

IV. If

IV.

If to the Seraglio you brought her,
    Where for flaves their maidens they fell,
I'm fure, tho' the Grand Seignior bought her,
    He'd foon turn a flave to La—l.

V.

Had I Hanover, Bremen, and Verden,
    And likewife the dutchy of Zell,
I'd part with them all for a farthing,
    To have my dear Molly La—l.

VI.

Or were I the King of Great Britain,
    To chufe a Minifter well,
And fupport the Throne that I fit on,
    I'd have under me Molly La—l.

VII.

Of all the bright beauties fo killing,
    In London's fair city that dwell,
None can give me fuch joy, were fhe willing,
    As the beautiful Molly La—l.

L 3   VIII. What

VIII.

What man would not give the great Ticket,
　　To his fhare if the benefit fell,
To be but one hour in a thicket,
　　With the beautiful Molly La—l.

IX.

Shou'd Venus now rife from the ocean,
　　And naked appear in her fhell,
She would not caufe half the emotion,
　　That we feel from dear Molly La—l.

X.

Old Orpheus, that hufband fo civil,
　　He follow'd his wife down to Hell,
And who would not go to the Devil,
　　For the fake of dear Molly La—l.

XI.

Her lips and her breath are much fweeter
　　Than the thing, which the Latins call Mel,
Who wou'd not thus pump for a meter,
　　To chyme to dear Molly La—l.

XII. In

XII.

In a bed you've feen pinks and rofes,
　　Wou'd you know a more delicate fmell,
Afk the fortunate man that repofes,
　　On the bofom of Molly La—l.

XIII.

'Tis a maxim moft fit for a lover,
　　If he kiffes he never fhould tell,
But no tongue can ever difcover
　　His pleafures with Molly La—l.

XIV.

Heaven keep our good King from a rifing,
　　But that rifing who's fitter to quell,
Than fome Lady with beauty furprifing,
　　And who fhou'd that be but La—l.

XV.

If Curll wou'd print me this fonnet,
　　To a volume my verfes fhou'd fwell,
A fig for what Dennis fays on it,
　　He can never find fault with La—l.

L 4　　　　　　　　　　XVI. Then

XVI.

Then Handel to mufic fhall fet it,
  Thro' England my ballad fhall fell,
And all the world readily get it,
  To fing to the praife of La—l.

A N O D E

TO WILLIAM PULTENEY, ESQ.

I.

REMOTE from Liberty and Truth,
By Fortune's crime, my early youth,
    Drank Error's poifon'd fprings ;
Taught by dark creeds, and myftic law,
Wrapp'd up in reverential awe,
    I bow'd to Priefts and Kings.

II.

Soon Reafon dawn'd, with troubled fight
I caught the glimpfe of painful light,
    Afflicted and afraid ;
Too weak it fhone to mark my way,
Enough to tempt my fteps to ftray,
    Along the dubious fhade.

III. Reftlefs

III.

Reftlefs I roam; when from afar,
Lo! Hooker fhines with friendly ftar,
  Sends forth a fteady ray;
Thus cheer'd, and eager to purfue,
I mount, till, glorious to my view,
  Locke fpreads the realms of day.

IV.

Now, warm'd with Sidney's noble page,
I pant with all the Patriot's rage,
  Nor wrapt in Plato's dream;
With More and Harrington, around
I tread fair Freedom's magic ground,
  And trace the flatt'ring fcheme.

V.

But foon the beauteous vifion flies,
And hideous fpectres ftrait arife,
  (Corruption's direful train)
The partial Judge perverting laws,
The Priefts forfaking Virtue's caufe,
  And Senates flaves to gain.

VI. Vainly

VI.

Vainly the pious Artift's toil
Would rear to Heaven a mortal pile,
   On fome immortal plan ;
Within a fhort tho' varying date,
Confin'd, alas! is every ftate
   Of empire and of man.

VII.

What tho' the good, the brave, the wife,
With adverfe force undaunted rife,
   To break th' eternal doom ;
Tho' Cato liv'd, tho' Tully fpoke,
And Brutus dealt the godlike ftroke,
   Yet perifh'd fated Rome.

VIII.

To fwell fome future tyrant's pride,
Tho' Fleury pours the golden tide
   On Gallia's fmiling fhores,
Once more her fields fhall thirft in vain,
For wholefome ftreams of honeft gain,
   Whilft Rapine waftes her ftores.

                                     IX. Yet

IX.

Yet glorious is the great defign,
And fuch, O Pulteney, fuch is thine,
  To prop a nation's frame;
If crufh'd beneath the facred weight,
The ruins of a falling State,
  Shall tell the Patriot's name.

THE SINECURE.

A POETICAL PETITION TO THE RIGHT HONOUR-
ABLE ROBERT WALPOLE, ESQ. FOR THE GO-
VERNMENT OF DUCK ISLAND IN ST. JAMES'S-
PARK.

WEARY'D with vain purfuits, and humble grown,
Sad in the country, and too poor for town;
Oh, how I long, in fome foft filent feat,
To tafte calm quiet, in ferene retreat!
Where books and eafe, and time for ferious thought,
May make Wit Wifdom e'er I'm good for nought.
Walpole, to thee the Mufe afflicted flies,
And, from the deep, like fhip-wreck'd Jonah—cries.
Thou, the right-hand of Fortune, form'd to give,
Let me not die, before I've learn'd to live.

      I not

I not for lordly poſt or penſion plead,
Sure Heaven will my reduc'd deſire ſucceed!
St. James's Wilderneſs, the Park's fair iſle,
Wou'd crown my wiſh, and Care's long hand beguile.
On that delightful and ſequeſter'd ſpot,
Fitted for me, as Zoar was for Lot:
I'd full content and ſatisfaction find,
And cultivate the garden of my mind;
Like good St. Evremont *, I'd grow a ſage,
And war with Nonſenſe, Vice, and Folly wage;
And, cabin'd ſafe in ſolitude and peace,
Think who's at helm, nor fear the ſtorm'd increaſe.
What princely pleaſure, in that envied ſcene,
To hold high empire o'er the people green?
Each roſy morn, the riſing Sun to wait,
And walk, with him, around my orb in ſtate;
My ſubject ducks ſhould watch my gracious will,
And paſſive geeſe ſhou'd owe me every quill;
To each in order traverſing my land,
I'd toſs due bleſſings with impartial hand.
Birds ſhou'd by love, and beaſt by fear, obey,
Yet all pay tribute in th' Imperial way;
Yet no tyrannic power ſhou'd pinch their right,
Nor bold Rebellion wing their wills for flight.

* Monſ. St. Evremont was preferred to the Government of
Duck Iſland, by King Charles the Second, and had a conſiderable
yearly penſion allowed him.

Still I'd adorn my state with something new,
Prune its wild profpects, and enlarge its view:
Mazes of knotty politics invent,
And in each open quarter plant content.
Then, when difpos'd for folitary thought,
Infpir'd by leifure, and by duty taught,
I'd run thro' Nature, and the caufes find,
Which lift fome fingle fouls above mankind;
Which, thro' defcending ages lengthen Fame,
And mark a Tully's, or a Walpole's name.
Kindling at this a still fublimer fire,
My grateful heart might teach me to afpire;
Smit with my Country's love, might Truth purfue,
And charm an unborn race, by painting you.
Exhauftlefs ftore my fubject ifle contains,
For apt illufions to adorn my ftrains!
In narrow compafs what is not compris'd,
Britannia's fea-girt land epitomiz'd;
From crowded fcenes of great Augufta rent,
As our blefs'd climate from the continent;
A colony of feather'd people, where,
(If we with great may fmaller things compare)
I like a Bifhop would o'er-fee my cure,
Or govern like a King—in miniature!
When my few friends to vifit me fhould pleafe,
How fweet to walk betwixt embowering trees;
Trees that fhould nod, obfervant, as I pafs,
And yield as humble homage as the grafs.

Or

Or, foft reclining in a fhort repofe,
Plucking furrounding fruitage as it grows;
I to thefe friends, inftructive—but not vain,
Wou'd, 'like St. John in Patmos, Truth explain;
Teach them that Happinefs in filence reigns,
And builds her bow'ry feats on peaceful plains.
While they tell news of mifchiefs hourly known
In public place, and the pernicious town,
And every word they fpeak confirms my own.
But fhou'd my patron deign to leave the Court,
And humbly to my hermitage refort;
Ambitious, I myfelf wou'd waft him o'er,
And hail his prefence on my happy fhore.
There might he fafe unbend his active mind,
Or form, perhaps, fome fcheme to blefs mankind:
Then wou'd the Golden Age be mine again,
And Charles's fhou'd be loft in George's reign.
How pleas'd in fancy, how do dreams delight,
And, ah! what pity mine fhou'd prove a rite!
Hear me, thou Atlas of our leaning State,
Confent at leaft to make one Poet great;
On thee the Mufes then fhall fix their eye,
And, for thy glory, whole Parnaffus vie;
To guard our hopes have been the Heroes pride,
'Tis good to have the Poets on thy fide.
I, for return, will yearly homage pay,
And blefs the rifing of thy natal day;

Not only this, but now and then afford
A trout, or duck, to dignify thy board.
'Tis done, I hear the royal mandate given,
Let Mitchell have his poor poetic Heaven;
And, to fupport his government, we grant
Twice fifty pounds per annum—all I want.
Pray fill the bowl—'tis decent to be glad,
Homer, on lefs occafion, had run mad.

FEMALE CHARACTERS.

Veluti in fpeculo.

THE chief in pride, Cardilla firft appears;
A flave to play, tho' wrinkled o'er with years;
Dupe to a reigning paffion for quadrille,
Her heart exults at fight of dear fpadille;
Thofe eyes, which fcarce within their orbits roll,
Beam a faint ray when Fortune gives a vole;
Eager and reftlefs fhe the game purfues,
And each fucceffive day the tafk renews:
Let old Cardilla, ere too late, attend
The fhort, but needful counfel of a friend—
Pack up your cards, the fhuffling paftime leave—
A few lifts more convey you to the grave.

Quite

Quite different scenes Matrona's thoughts engage,
Scenes that adorn, support, and gladden Age;
In Wisdom's paths with calm delight she treads,
And o'er Distress the tear of Pity sheds;
Nor only sheds a tear—her hand supplies
The orphan's wants, and wipes the widow's eyes:
Unfeigned Virtue all her actions guides,
Glows in her heart, and o'er her steps presides;
Meek and resign'd, with fortitude she bears
The pains of Nature, and the load of years,
Looks back with pleasure on each well spent day,
And forward to the tomb without dismay.

Pratella's fav'rite weapon is her tongue,
Oil'd like a hone, and like a balance hung;
Once put in motion quick vibration keeps,
And scarcely is at rest ev'n while she sleeps—
Did Wit or Wisdom her harangues inspire,
We then could hear with patience, and admire;
But what her pert, loquacious tongue employs,
Is Folly, Fashion, Scandal, Trash and Noise:
Envy and Spleen reign jointly in her breast,
Of all the softer passions dispossest;
Envy depreciates every generous deed,
And makes ev'n Virtue like a victim bleed,
While Spleen beholds, with telescopic eyes,
The smallest faults, and swells them into Vice,

In

In heighten'd colours ev'ry foible draws,
And holds from modeſt Worth its juſt applauſe—
Go, look at home in calm Reflection's glaſs,
And on yourſelf an honeſt cenſure paſs!
A ſov'reign cure, Pratella, there you'll find,
To heal a venom'd tongue, and ranc'rous mind.

Not ſuch Modeſta: when ſhe deigns to ſpeak,
Truth guides her tongue, and Beauty warms her cheek;
The native muſic of her voice imparts
Grace to her words, and pleaſure to our hearts:
The wiſeſt maxims of the hoary ſage
(With care ſelected from the Stoic page)
Enrich her mind, and give her language weight,
In friendly converſe, or in learn'd debate;
Her ſpeech no love of Scandal e'er betrays,
Modeſta's ſilent when ſhe cannot praiſe:
When Wit and Mirth their lively charms diſplay,
Her genius ſparkles, and her ſoul is gay;
No prudiſh frowns upon her face appears,
And in her conduct no coquetiſh airs;
Courteous to all, unconſcious of offence,
She ſhines the firſt in Virtue, Truth and Senſe.

Young, briſk and bold, Vanetta flaunts away,
And would be thought the gayeſt of the gay;
Yet Summer-flies receive more gaudy hues
From Sol's warm radiance, and Aurora's dews:

Full

Full she displays, in every public place,
Her pride of heart, and impudence of face;
She mimics Wit, while Folly mimics her,
And hard to say, which mimic to prefer:
Like Milton's Death, she " grins a ghastly smile,"
Much too forbidding ever to beguile,
And yet Vanetta deems her self-lov'd charms
Of power to draw the wealthiest to her arms.
Grant that success her fondest wishes crowns!
Not Hymen's raptures will unbend her frowns.
To church she goes, with most affected zeal,
Not to confess her faults, but to conceal;
Thoughtless of Heav'n, she hurries thro' her pray'rs,
Eyes her dear self, and then around her stares:
But if, perchance, on Pride the Parson treats,
She drops her bible, flirts her fan, and frets;
So the gall'd jade is seen to wince and start,
If you but gently touch the tender part.

Unlike Vanetta is that charming maid,
Whose beauty needs no fashionable aid,
Amanda nam'd—to low but honest birth,
Her modest mien and solid sense give worth;
She leaves to those, whom fickle Fancy bred,
The rainbow ribbon, and the high rais'd head:
In this lov'd Nymph are beauteously combin'd
The decent dress and well instructed mind:

The

The church fhe vifits, but without parade,
And there her vows religioufly are paid;
She fears no cenfure when the Prieft declaims,
Whofe life is virtuous, and fincere her aims:
Amanda's feet in pious paths have trod,
Which lead to honour, fafety, peace, and God.
Vanetta, view this lovely picture well,
And ftrive, in all that's good, Amanda to excel!

EPIGRAM.

TOM prais'd his friend (who chang'd his ftate)
For binding faft himfelf and Kate
    In union fo divine;
Wedlock's the end of life, he cried.
Too true, alas! faid Jack, and figh'd——
    ——'Twill be the end of mine.

EPIGRAM.

SAYS my Lord to his cook, you fon of a punk,
How comes it I fee you, thus, ev'ry day drunk?
Phyficians, they fay, once a month do allow,
A man for his health, to get drunk—as a fow.
That is right, quoth the cook, but the day they don't
    fay,
So for fear I fhould mifs it, I'm drunk ev'ry day.

ODE

O D E

TO LORD EDGECUMBE'S PIG.

YE Mufes quit your facred ftream,
   And aid me like the bard of yore,
Hight, Milton, for like his, my theme
   In verfe was never fung before.
Indeed the tale is often told in profe;
Since all the world the mighty wonder knows!

Theme of fublimity! my boar,
   All hail! thou beaft of high renown,
As famous as the horfe of yore,
   That won his lucky Lord a crown *;
Fam'd as Mifs Lefbia's bird, in verfe fo foft
Recorded, or the rabbits of Moll Toft!

Hail pig! at Tunbridge born and bred,
   Who fingleft out his L——p there,
Event that round the region fpread,
   And made the gaping million ftare;
And ftrange it was to fee, upon my word,
A pig for ever trotting with my L—d!

* Darius.

The

The gentry marvell'd at the fight;
   The public walks, the rooms they rung:
'Twas L—d and pig from morn to night,
   And pig and L———p all day long.
Soon did the wond'rous tale to London wing,
The nobles heard it, and they told the King.

Good Lord! says one, what can this mean?
   And rais'd the whites of both his eyes:
It bodes some dire portent I ween.
   I can't tell, sure, a second cries.
Thus did the world indulge conjecture vague,
For earthquakes some contending, some a plague!

But such the meaner world, the crew
   Of dull uneducated brains;
But mark th' opinions of the few,
   Hear what the learned world maintains:
Some deem'd the L—d St. Anthony incog.
To earth re-travell'd with his fav'rite hog.

Others, in Oriental lore
   Deep vers'd, that heard the peerless tale,
Declar'd with judgment sage, the boar
   Did secrets to my Lord reveal,
Like the fam'd Dove the Muffelman's revere,
Which, billing, whisper'd in the Prophet's * ear.

      * Mahomet.

               While

While some as sagely as the rest,
    Who firm believ'd in transmigrations,
Pronounc'd this friendly grunting beast
    One of his Lordship's near relations,
Doom'd by the Fates, for certain deeds divine,
To animate the body of a swine!

Hail pighog! by whose potent aid,
    My L—d his health had, and employ!
My L—y too, was brought-to-bed,
    Heav'n bless it! of a chopping boy.
Event that Fame so founded with her horn,
As scar'd the very infants yet unborn!

Thrice happy hog! with Mrs. Joan *,
    Who, in a chariot, cheek by jole,
Did'st, Jehu-like, from Tunbridge Town
    To Mount's enchanting mansions roll:
Where to thy levee, thousands did repair.
With nine fat Aldermen and Mr. Mayor.

The Mayor and Aldermen polite,
    Swore that without or fee or purchase,
If so his Lordship thoft it right,
    They'd choose thee, gentle swine, for burgess.
Thank ye, replied his Lordship; but, odsnigs!
Tho' asses fit, 'tis never granted pigs.

    * My Lady's waiting woman.

                   Thrice

Thrice happy hog! who lov'ſt to ſnore,
    Reclining on my L—y's lap,
Who gives thy hiſt'ry o'er and o'er,
    While pigſnye gruntling takes his nap.
Delightful tale, that ſtrikes all ſtories dumb,
From Gog, the mighty giant, to Tom Thumb.

TO A LADY WHO GREATLY ADMIRED THE SPANISH POETRY.

IN THE MANNER OF ALONZO DE ERCILLA.

WHEN I would thy beauties paint,
All the pow'r of verſe is faint;
Though a hapleſs, hopeleſs Lover,
All thy charms I can diſcover;
Charms are only found in thee,
Charms which 'tis unſafe to ſee;
Charms which might a Hermit bribe;
Charms no language can deſcribe.
Where words no fit ideas raiſe,
Silence beſt expreſſes praiſe.

But when I explore thy mind,
A new world of charms I find;

Every

Every virtue, every grace,
There poffefs their proper place ;
When of thefe I think awhile,
Raptures foon my foul beguile.
For too ftrong, too clear a light,
Suits not either fenfe or fight !
All we can do is to gaze,
Sweetly loft in fond amaze.

Faireft Flavia, fav'rite maid !
Let thefe artlefs lays perfuade.
Not that I am fkill'd in verfe,
Or thy conquefts can rehearfe ;
But, what I did long conceal,
That thy beauty's force I feel,
And in mournful numbers figh,
For thofe charms by which I die.
Let them tell—what would you more ?—
That I expire, and yet adore.

ON THE ROYAL MARRIAGE ACT.

QUOTH Dick to Tom, this act appears
 Abfurd, as I'm alive ;
To take the crown at eighteen years,
 The wife at twenty-five.

The

The myft'ry how fhall we explain?
  For, fure, as * Dowdefwell faid,
Thus early if they're.fit to *reign*,
  They muft be fit to *wed!*

Quoth Tom to Dick—thou art a fool,
  And little know'ft of life!
Alas! 'tis eafier far to rule
  A kingdom than a wife.

AN EMBLEM OF WEDLOCK.

IN CHAUCER's STYLE.

FULL well by lerned clerkis it is fed,
" That womanhood for mannis ufe was made :"
Yet naughty man liketh not one or fo ;
But lufteth, aye, unthriftily, for mo.
And whom he whilom cherifhyd whan tied
By holy church, he can not her abide.
Like to a dog, that lighteth of a bone,
His tail he waggeth, glad thereof ygrown ;
But if thilk bone unto his tail thou tie,
Bardie, he, fearing it, away doth fly.

* Mr. Dowdefwell's Speech on the Royal Marriage Act.

A SHORT POETICAL DESCRIPTION OF A FEMALE ROUTE.

BEHOLD the scene a motley tribe compose,
Wives, widows, maids, and intermingle beaux:
All orders, ages, in one league unite;
And to dear passage consecrate the night!
Now the dice rattle in the sounding box,
Now groans the table with repeated knocks,
(Delightful music to the gamester's ear)
While ev'ry bosom beats with hope or fear.
A pass resounds;—what wond'rous transports rise
In Cælia's breast, and lightens in her eyes!
She sweeps the board—the fop with ardent gaze,
Admires the beauty that her arm displays.

But who, unmov'd, can bear the piteous sight,
While Cynthia frets, and raves at Fortune's spite?
Fled from her cheeks are every love and grace,
And all the Fury threatens in her face:
Distracted, lost with grief, and rage o'ercome,
She quits the dice, and flies to storm at home.

When I a curse implore, may courteous Fate
With such a consort curse the man I hate!—
But, if there's one amongst the many found,
Adorn'd with Modesty, with Reason crown'd,

Who

Who treads the flippery paths of Youth with care,
And, uninfected, breathes in tainted air :
If fuch there be, kind Heav'n afford thy aid,
And foften to my wifh the virtuous maid !

THE FOUR FOLLOWING EPIGRAMS WERE WRIT-
TEN BY MR. JOHN HACKETT, FORMERLY OF
BALIOL COLLEGE.

A Cock within a ftable pent,
 Was ftrutting o'er fome heaps of dung,
And, ay, as round and round he went,
 The mettl'd courfers ftampt and flung.
Bravo ! quoth he, a decent noife,
 We make a tolerable pother ;
But let's take care, my merry boys,
 We tread not upon one another.

FRANK, who will any friend fupply,
Lent me ten pieces. Frank, fays I,
Haft any paper ? 'Tis but fair,
You take my note. Quoth Frank, hold there ;
Jack, to the cafh I've bid adieu,
No need to wafte my paper too.

WHEN fancies queer plagu'd Menelaus' head,
Thus to her Lord, the blooming Helen said,—
This earthly part to Troy tho' Paris bore,
Still was my foul with thee, on Sparta's shore.
Troth it may be, quoth he, I believe it well;
Howe'er, the next time leave me the body, Nell,

TO MR. W————.

FROM morning to evening, and evening to morn-
    ing,
Your fellows are peft'ring us with their French horn-
    ing;
Do, ftop this damn'd work : you forget your friend
    Joe ;
Your horns, Sir, made noife enough three years
    ago,

ON THE DEATH OF THE LADY OF THE RIGHT
HONOURABLE JOHN SHELLY, WHO DIED IN
CHILD-BED.

BY THE REV. DR. DELAP.

TEARS, such as Angels weep, shou'd now diffuse,
Around this hallow'd earth, their holiest dews,
Where rest fair Wilhelmina's last remains.
She for her infant bore a mother's pains,
And died to give it life.   In Beauty's bloom,
Heav'n snatch'd its favourite to an early tomb;
Its gent'lest, best belov'd, who seem'd design'd
To shew how far a meek and modest mind,
With its own simple pow'rs and native grace,
Could mend the features of the fairest face;
How fix a friend's, a brother's, husband's love,
Beyond, alas, the pow'r of Death to move!

Self-tutor'd thus, above all rules of Art,
This child of Nature play'd her blameless part,
And sunk with that unsullied soul to rest,
Which Heav'n first breath'd into her infant breast.

M 3   THE

THE WAY TO CHUSE A WIFE.

IF e'er I quit the single life,
Be this the model of my wife—
A Beauty, without Art, compleat,
Who's from her toilet *simply neat*;
Who golden tissue can despise,
And wears no brilliants, but her eyes;
Desiring Love, and sparkling Wit,
Soft blended in her eyes should meet;
And, in her dimpled smiles be seen
A modest, with a cheerful mien.

As pauses find in music place,
Her speech let proper silence grace;
Her conversation ever free
From censure, as from levity;
And undissembled innocence,
Not apt to give or take offence;
Nor fond of compliments, nor rude;
Not a coquet, nor yet a prude;
Averse to wanton serenades,
Nor pleas'd with midnight masquerades.
The virtues that her sex adorn,
By *honour* guarded, not by *scorn*;

Not

Not fuperftitious, nor profane,
But in Religion greatly plain.
To fuch a virgin, fuch a wife,
I give my love, I give my life.

O N L O V E.

AN ELEGY.

BY DR. AKENSIDE.

Too much my heart of Beauty's power hath known,
Too long to Love hath Reafon left her throne ;
Too long my Genius mourn'd his myrtle chain,
And three rich years of youth confum'd in vain.
My wifhes, lull'd with foft inglorious dreams,
Forgot the Patriot's and the Sage's themes ;
Thro' each Elyfian vale and Fairy grove,
Thro' all th' enchanted paradife of Love,
Mifled by fickly Hope's deceitful flame,
Averfe to Action, and renouncing Fame.

At laft the vifionary feenes decay,
My eyes exulting blefs the new-born day,
Whofe faithful beams detect the dangerous road
In which my heedlefs feet fecurely trode,

M 4   And

And ſtrip the phantoms of their lying charms,
That lur'd my ſoul from Wiſdom's peaceful arms.

For ſilver ſtreams and banks beſpread with flow'rs,
For moſſy couches and harmonious bowers,
Lo! barren heaths appear, and pathleſs woods,
And rocks hung dreadful o'er unfathom'd floods:
For openneſs of heart, for tender ſmiles,
Looks fraught with love, and wrath-diſarming wiles,
Lo! ſullen Spight, and perjur'd Luſt of Gain,
And cruel Pride, and crueller Diſdain.
Lo! cordial faith to ideot airs refin'd,
Now coolly civil, now tranſporting kind.
For graceful eaſe, lo! Affectation walks,
And dull half ſenſe, for Wit and Wiſdom talks.
New to each hour what low delight ſucceeds,
What precious furniture of hearts and heads!
By nought their prudence, but by getting known;
And all their courage in deceiving ſhown.

See next what plagues attend the Lover's ſtate,
What frightful forms of Terror, Scorn, and Hate!
See burning Fury Heaven and Earth defy!
See dumb Deſpair in icy fetters lie!
See black Suſpicion bend his gloomy brow,
The hideous image of himſelf to view;

And

And fond Belief, with all a Lover's flame,
Sinks in those arms that point his head with shame!
There wan Dejection, falt'ring as he goes,
In shades and silence vainly seeks repose;
Musing thro' pathless wilds, consumes the day,
Then, lost in darkness, weeps the hours away.
Here the gay croud of Luxury advance,
Some touch the lyre, and others urge the dance;
On every head the rosy garland glows,
In every hand the golden goblet flows.
The Syren views them with exulting eyes,
And laughs at bashful Virtue as she flies.
But see behind, where Scorn and Want appear,
The grave remonstrance, and the witty sneer.
See fell Remorse in action, prompt to dart
Her snaky poison thro' the conscious heart.
And Sloth to cancel, with oblivious shame,
The fair memorial of recording Fame.
Are these delights that one would wish to gain?
Is this th' Elysium of a sober brain?
To wait for happiness in female smiles,
Bear all her scorn, be caught with all her wiles,
With prayers, with bribes, with lies her pity crave,
Bless her hard bonds, and boast to be her slave;
To feel, for trifles, a distracted train
Of hopes and terrors equally in vain;

This

This hour to tremble, and the next to glow,
Can Pride, can Senfe, can Reafon ftoop fo low ?
When Virtue, at an eafier price, difplays
The facred wreaths of honourable praife ;
When Wifdom utters her divine decree,
To laugh at pompous Folly, and be free.

I bid adieu, then, to thefe woeful fcenes ;
I bid adieu to all the fex of Queens ;
Adieu to every fuffering, fimple foul,
That lets a woman's will his eafe controul.
There laugh, ye witty, and rebuke, ye grave !
For me, I fcorn to boaft that I'm a flave.
I bid the whining brotherhood be gone.
Joy to my heart ! my wifhes are my own !
Farewel the female Heaven, the female Hell ;
To the great God of Love a glad farewel.
Is this the triumph of thy awful name ?
Are thefe the fplendid hopes that urg'd thy aim,
When firft my bofom own'd thy haughty fway,
When thus Minerva heard thee, boafting fay :

" Go, martial maid, elfewhere thy arts employ,
" Nor hope to fhelter that devoted boy.
" Go, teach the folemn fons of Care and Age,
" The penfive Statefman, and the midnight Sage ;
" The young, with me, muft other leffons prove,
" Youth calls for Pleafure, Pleafure calls for Love.
                                        " Behold

" Behold his heart thy grave advice difdains,
" Behold, I bind him in eternal chains."

Alas! great Love, how idle was the boaft!
Thy chains are broken, and thy leffons loft.
Thy wilful rage has tir'd my fuffering heart,
And Paffion, Reafon forc'd thee to depart.

But wherefore doft thou linger on thy way:
Why vainly fearch for fome pretence to ftay,
When crouds of vaffals court thy pleafing yoke,
And countlefs victims bow beneath the ftroke?
Lo! round thy fhrine a thoufand youths advance,
Warm with the gentle ardours of Romance;
Each longs t' affert thy caufe with feats of arms,
And make the world confefs Dulcinea's charms.
Ten thoufand girls, with flow'ry chaplets crown'd,
To groves and ftreams thy tender triumph found;
Each bids the ftream in murmurs fpeak her flame,
Each calls the grove to figh her fhepherd's name.
But if thy pride fuch eafy honour fcorn,
If nobler trophies muft thy toil adorn,
Behold yon flow'ry antiquated maid,
Bright in the bloom of threefcore years difplay'd;
Her thou fhalt bind in thy delightful chains,
And thrill with gentler pangs her wither'd veins,
Her frofty cheek with crimfon blufhes dye,
With dreams of rapture melt her maudlin eye.

M 6   Turn

Turn then thy labours to the fervile croud,
Entice the wary, and controul the proud;
Make the fad Mifer his beft gains forego,
The folemn Statefman figh to be a beau.
The bold Coquette with fondeft paffion burn,
The Bacchanalian o'er his bottle mourn :
And that chief glory of thy pow'r maintain,
" To poize Ambition in a female brain."
Be thefe thy triumphs, but no more prefume
That my rebellious heart will yield thee room.
I know thy puny force, thy fimple wiles ;
I break triumphant thro' thy flimfey toils ;
I fee thy dying lamp's laft languid glow,
Thy arrows blunted, and unbrac'd thy bow.
I feel diviner fires my breaft inflame,
To active Science, and ingenuous Fame :
Refume the paths my earlieft choice began,
And lofe, with pride, the Lover in the Man.

ODE TO VENUS, ON OPENING THE PANTHEON.

BY A YOUNG LADY OF FASHION.

[Imitated from Horace]

BRIGHT Venus, Covent-Garden's queen,
Forfake awhile each hackney'd fcene,

For

For fomething new and rare;
And, quitting Luft's confin'd abode,
Bid Thomas drive to Oxford Road,
    And feek a purer air.

From Nelfon's, Hayes's and Soho,
And Frere's * politer bagnio,
    To yon gay Temple rove;
There lavifh all your winning arts,
To catch our purfes, or our hearts,
    And give a loofe to Love.

Libations, lo! to thee are made,
Of capillaire and lemonade,
    And juice of cooling tea;
Whole hecatombs of bifcuits rife,
Beaux, bawds, and bifhops, mingle fighs,
    To facrifice to thee.

Bright Goddefs hafte, and with thee take
The modifh Macaroni Rake,
    Who Fafhion's law reveres;
Array'd, as her caprice decrees,
In coat a yard above his knees,
    And curls above his ears.

* The Coterie.

Soft

Soft foother of the bed of Care,
Let wanton Coxe attend thee there,
   For Diffipation made ;
Her manners open, free, and kind,
Her heaving bofom unconfin'd,
   By whalebone or brocade.

Lead Vigour, lufty child of Health,
More coveted than birth or wealth,
   By all who wifh to pleafe ;
Without whofe falutary grace,
The rapture-feigning Fop's embrace,
   Is but a pow'r to *teize.*

THE FOLLOWING EPIGRAM WAS WRITTEN BY
G. A. SELWYN, ESQ. ON FINDING A PAIR OF
SHOES ON THE BED OF ONE OF THE FEMALE
MEMBERS OF THE COTERIE.

WELL may Sufpicion fhake its head,
  Well may Clarinda's fpoufe be jealous,
When the dear wanton takes to bed
  Her very *fhoes*—becaufe they're *fellows.*

                       ON

ON A LATE MARRIAGE.

FROM flavifh, mean dependance rais'd
  By man's capricious love ;
With richeft filks, and ruffles grac'd,
  Now view Dorinda move.

The home-fpun ftuffs fhe us'd to wear,
  And us'd to patch and mend,
Are now unworthy of her care,
  She's got a better friend.

Time was fhe earn'd her daily bread,
  And walk'd the ftreets in pattens,
But now fhe dreffes up her head,
  And ftruts abroad in fatins.

A C A T C H,

TO A COMPANY OF BAD FIDDLE-SCRAPERS.

" To the Tune of Water parted from the Sea."

MAY ye never play in tune,
  In the morning, night, or noon :
May you ne'er at noon or night,
  Know the wrong end from the right.

May

May the ftrings be ever breaking,
    Pegs, I charge ye, ne'er unfcrew;
May your heads be always aching,
    Till the fiddle's broke in two.

MR. HEDGES TO SIR HANS SLOANE.

SINCE you, dear Doctor, fav'd my life,
By turns to blefs and curfe my wife;
In confcience I'm obliged to do,
What your commands enjoin'd me to:
According then to your command,
That I fhould fearch the Weftern land,
And fend you all that I can find
Of curious things of every kind;
I've ravag'd air, earth, fea and caverns,
Wine, women, children, tombs and taverns;
And greater rarities can fhew,
Than Grefham's children ever knew;
Which carrier Dick fhall bring you down,
Next time the waggon comes to town.

    Firft, I have drops of the fame fhower,
Which Jove in Danae's lap did pour;
From Carthage brought, the fword I'll fend,
That help'd Queen Dido to her end:

                                    The

The ſnake ſkin, which, you may believe,
The ſerpent caſt who tempted Eve:
A fig-leaf apron, 'tis the ſame
Which Adam wore to hide his ſhame;
But now wants darning: Sir, beſide,
The jaw by which poor Abel died;
A whetſtone worn exceeding ſmall,
Which Time has whet his teeth withal.
The pigeon ſtuft, which Noah ſent,
To tell which way the water went—
A ring I've got of Samſon's hair,
The ſame which Delilah did wear.
St. Dunſtan's tongs, as ſtory goes,
That pinch'd the Devil by the noſe.
The very ſhaft, as all may ſee,
Which Cupid ſhot at Anthony:
And what beyond them all I prize,
A glance of Cleopatra's eyes.
Some ſtrains of eloquence which hung,
In Roman times, on Tully's tongue;
Which long conceal'd and loſt had lain,
Till Cowper found them out again!
Then I've (moſt curious to be ſeen)
A ſcorpion's bite to cure the ſpleen.
As More cures worms in ſtomach bred,
I've pills cure maggots in the head:
With the receipt how you may make 'em,
To you I leave the time to take 'em.

I've got a ray of Phœbus' shine,
Found in the bottom of a mine!
A Lawyer's conscience, large and clear,
Fit for a Judge himself to wear.
I've choice of nostrums, how to make
An oath which Churchmen will not take.
In a thumb vial you shall see,
Close stopt, some drops of honesty;
Which, after searching kingdoms round,
At last was in a cottage found.
I han't collected any care,
Of that there's plenty every-where:
But, after wond'rous labour spent,
I've got three grains of rich content.
It is my wish, it is my glory,
To furnish your nicknackatory:
I only beg that when you shew 'em,
You'll fairly tell to whom you owe 'em;
Which will your future patients teach
To do, as has done yours,

T. H.

THE WALDEN HUNT.

LET dull politicians eternally prate,
And leave their own business for that of the State,

For

For bold Britiſh Liberty tread on the laws,
And think the worſt men may ſupport the beſt cauſe;
Let them ſwell high to Freedom the generous ſong,
And be madmen themſelves, when a Miniſter's wrong;
Truſt their lives and their fortunes to bankrupts alone;
And prove themſelves loyal, by blaming the Throne;
That our fooliſh diſſentions may happily ceaſe,
Let them hourly attempt a new ſtab at our peace,
And rail at all others as villains or ſlaves,
Who doubt once the virtue of beggars and knaves;
But engag'd by the manly delights of the chace,
Where health and where pleaſure hold equally pace,
The Walden keen ſportſmen ſhall ſwell up my ſtrain,
As they follow the lightning-ſwift ſtag o'er the plain,
With rapture's own muſic awake the ſweet morn,
And kindle freſh joys at the ſound of the horn.

On Friday the third, leaving ſea-coal and ſin,
For Walden we flew to the Roſe and Crown Inn;
From whence, the next morning, to Gardener's * we
    rode,
And reach'd in high ſpirits, his welcome abode;
Where the well-meaning coxcomb, half hoſt and half
    friend,
Who loves, what we love, and ne'er minds what we
    ſpend;

* The Crown at Cheſterford.

With

With a chearful *bark forward* receiv'd the whole party,
And fwore out his pleafure to find us all hearty.
The hounds, in the morning, led on by Will Deane,
And the hunt fmartly drefs'd in their general green,
We threw off ev'ry day, without puppy or lac'd coat,
Tho' Gard'ner frown'd hard at our collar and waift-
  coat.
Throughout the whole chace Phœbus fmil'd on our
  way,
And each ftag gave us hard, but gave excellent play ;
High rearing his antlers, and fcorning to yield,
He fhot thro' the thicket, or fcour'd o'er the field ;
But in vain did he labour to leave us behind,
The hounds and the hunters kept pace with the wind.
The good-natur'd M—ifh tho' willing to fpare,
Now pierc'd with his fhouts thro' the echoing air ;
And, quite a keen fportfman, no longer drew back,
But boldly rode up at the head of the pack.
The two jolly brothers, Sir James and young L—g,
Prefs'd eagerly forward to lead the whole throng ;
With a gen'rous ambition inflam'd at the fight,
But Ki—c-te, who madden'd thro' actual delight,
Pufh'd Blower fo hard that he panted for breath,
Tho' a horfe who is chiefly firft in at the death.
The Major, with L—ge, and Sir Ferdinand then,
Spurr'd on, and behav'd themfelves nobly like men ;
        While

While both the Be—nqu—ts whipp'd smarter and
 smarter,
And W-lk-fon did almoft wonders with Tartar;
To keep with the foremoft feem'd L——ke's warm
 view,
And L——ler the Feather amazingly flew;
But the poor Chefnut gelding ran foon to a ftop,
And Death, that grim horfeman, thro' envy feiz'd
 Crop * ;
Here alfo fhould L—bock with credit be nam'd,
Tho' his horfe was fo quick, and fo curfedly lam'd;
And timber-to'd Billy † too merits a line,
Tho' he twice fpill'd his mafter, and fell with poor
 V—ne;
But Th-nt-n the chubby was very much mifs'd,
For the fellow's a favourite quite with our lift;
And all wifh'd for Oliver's fpirit and fong,
With whom time ftill lengthens, yet never feems long;
Nor could we but fome glaring anger betray,
At the abfence of N—ve and his titupping grey;
Yet chiefly a Nymph || let us gratefully praife,
Who grac'd the gay concourfe of one of our days;
Like another Diana, the Woodland's fair Queen,
Purfu'd the ftout ftag with the brothers in green;
At hedge-row, or river, ne'er trembling ftood,
But clear'd the high brake, or plung'd deep in the flood;

* Mr. L——ke's horfe.   † Mr. V's horfe.
|| A Lady who rode the whole day with the hunt.

That

That the charmer was Cynthia at first we believ'd,
But we look'd at her eyes, and were soon undeceiv'd;
The keen killing glance was all passion and fire,
And promis'd to bless, while it rais'd up desire;
The ripe rosy lip, that provok'd the long kiss,
Prepar'd to return, what was paid it, in bliss,
And the warm flesh and blood of the form all display'd
The kind hearted girl, not the surly old maid.—
Each day having pull'd the stag joyously down,
To Ruffee's we return, at the Rose and the Crown,
Where M—tish politeness, and laughter preside,
And Friendship disdains to know Party or Pride;—
Then while honest Partridge took charge of expence,
Our toasts were all guided by humour and sense;
In Pope's happy thought, on the bottle and bowl;
Sat the true feast of reason, and the true flow of soul;
And the glass, as it should do, went cheerfully round,
To heighten our pleasure, and not to confound—
All satisfied here, the delights of the field,
To other enjoyments, in course, were to yield;
A change the most wise that our sages can find,
Both a pleasant and timely relief to the mind—
We therefore return'd, when we wish'd it, to town,
In just the same humour as when we went down;
Determin'd, since life but few pleasures can give,
To seize all in turn, and *to live while we live.*

HOR.

HOR. LIB. I. ODE 38, IMITATED.

PERSICOS ODI, &c.

DEAR Jenny, to confefs my mind,
 I never yet could bear,
To fee the lovely maid I priz'd
By ev'ry greafy prig difguis'd,
 With powder and falfe hair.

Be cleanlinefs thy morning care,
 Nor covet Art's attire,
In native elegance compleat,
You look as fair, and kifs as fweet,
 As Love and I defire.

THERON, among his travels, found
A broken ftatue on the ground,
And fearching onward as he went,
He trac'd a ruin'd monument.
Mould, mofs, and fhades had overgrown
The fculpture of the mould'ring ftone,
Yet, ere he pafs'd, with much ado,
He guefs'd, and fpelt out Scipio.

        Enough!

Enough! he cried! I'll drudge no more
In turning the dull fages o'er,
Let Pedants wafte their hours of eafe,
To pore all night o'er Socrates;
And feed their boys with notes and rules,
Thofe tedious recipes of fchools;
To cure Ambition, I can learn
With greater eafe, the great concern
Of mortals, how we may defpife
All the gay things below the fkies.

Methinks, a mould'ring pyramid
Says all that the old Sages faid:
For me, thefe fhattered tombs contain
More morals than the Vatican;
The duft of heroes, caft abroad,
And kick'd and trampl'd on the road,
The relicts of a lofty mind,
That lately wars and crowns defign'd,
Toft for a jeft, from wind to wind,
Bids me be humble, and forbear,
Dull monuments of Fame to rear,
They are but caftles in the air.
The tow'ring height, and frightful falls,
The ruin'd heaps and funerals,
Of fmoaking kingdoms, and their Kings,
Tell me a thoufand mournful things

In melancholy filence—He,
That living, could not bear to fee
An equal, now lies torn and dead ;
Here his pale trunk, and there his head.
Great Pompey, while I meditate,
With folemn horror thy fad fate,
Thy carcafe fcatter'd on the fhore,
Without a name! inftructs me more
Than my whole library before !

   Lie ftill, my Plutarch, then, and fleep ;
And, my good Seneca, may keep
Your volumes clofs'd for ever too,
I have no farther ufe for you ;
For when I feel my virtue fail,
And my ambitious thoughts prevail,
I'll take a turn among the tombs,
And fee whereto all glory comes !
There the vile foot of ev'ry flave
Infults a Charles, or a Guftave !
Beggars with awful afhes fport,
And tread the Cæfars in the dirt.

A PARODY.

BY FRANCIS LORD VERULAM,

THE world's a bubble, and the life of man,
     lefs than a fpan ;
In his conceptions wretched, from the womb,
      - fo to the tomb :
Curs'd from the cradle, and brought up to years
     with cares and fears.
Who then to frail mortality fhall truft,
But limns the water, or but writes in duft.
Yet fince with forrow here we live oppreft,
     What life is beft ?
Courts are but only fuperficial fchools,
     to dandle fools :
The rural parts are turn'd into a den
     of favage men.
And where's a city from all vice fo free,
But may be term'd the worft of all the three ?
Domeftic cares afflict the hufband's bed,
     Or pains his head :
Thofe who live fingle take it for a curfe,
     or do things worfe.
Some would have children, thofe that have them, none,
     or wifh them gone.
What is it then to have, or have no wife,
But fingle thraldom, or a double ftrife !

         Our

Our own affections ftill at home to pleafe,
          Is a difeafe ;
To crofs the fea to any foreign foil,
         perils and toil ;
Wars with their noife affright us ; when they ceafe
        We're worfe in Peace.
What then remains, but that we ftill fhould cry,
Not to be born, or, being born, to die.

HOR. BOOK I. ODE XXIII.

Vitas hinnuleo me fimilis, Chloe,
Quærenti, &c.

WHY, (Chloe, like the tender fawn,
That trembling fcuds acrofs the lawn,
 To feek its anxious doe ;
That ftarts and pricks its little ears,
And raifes all a mother's fears)
 Doft thou thus coynefs fhow ?

Why fly me with fuch furious hafte,
As if on Lybia's burning wafte
 Thou'dft met a tyger wan ?
Full big art thou to hang about,
And play with Mamma's petticoat,
 Whofe charms are ripe for man.

        THE

THE CAUSE OF INCONSTANCY.

How have I heard the Fair lament
 Man's falfhood, and their wretched fate!
How few are with their fpoufe content,
 Or conftant to their fighing mate!

How feldom fouls below are join'd,
 For one another form'd above!
How feldom pairs of hearts we find,
 By Heaven ordain'd for mutual love!

Thus man's inconftant foul we blame,
 For want of knowledge, or of thought,
When all the while, 'tis in the frame
 Of both their bodies lies the fault.

When Jove had made this little ball,
 For four-legg'd beafts, and creeping things,
At length he form'd, to govern all,
 A two-legg'd creature without wings.

Millions of thefe he made at once,
 To fave himfelf all further trouble,
And men and women, for the nonce,
 By pairs, like tallies, he made double.

Then

Then from Olympus' dreadful top,
  Well shaken in a bag together,
He tofs'd them down, and let them drop,
  Juft as it pleas'd the wind and weather.

Some fell in Afia, fome in Greece,
  In England fome, and fome in Spain;
But feldom two of the fame piece,
  In the fame climate met again.

Hence men, who grown to riper years,
  Rememb'ring this their former making,
Hunt up and down to find their peers,
  And women too, in the fame taking.

Some prove too fhort, and fome too tall,
  This is too big, and that too little,
A fault they're fure to find in all,
  Few ever tally to a tittle.

By chance a pair may meet and love,
  And fpend their lives in blifs together;
But when they tumbled from above,
  It muft be mighty temperate weather.

From hence the murmuring fair may fee,
  Men's hearts are not to blame a-bit,
Our fouls would never difagree,
  If once our bodies did but fit.

AN

A N O D E,

WRITTEN A FEW DAYS BEFORE THE LONG
COLLEGE·VACATION, 1763.

BY MR. HARTIS.

COME, thou laughter-loving power,
Goddefs of the feftive hour,
Blue-ey'd Mirth, and bring along
Gamefome fport, and jocund fong;
Wit with native humour warm,
Converfation's lively charm,
And yet more, to ope the foul,
Bring, O bring the jovial bowl.
Let us lift the gladfome fhout,
Let us wake the midnight rout,
Brifkly let us all advance
In the fprightly-woven dance!
Every deed on every fide,
Let the foul of rapture guide.
Care begone! and grief adieu
What have ye with joy to do?
And thou too, that lov'ft to dwell
Mufing in the penfive cell,
Heavenly queen of piercing eye,
Farewel fweet Philofophy!

What

What if thou with hermit-look,
From Retirement's fartheſt nook,
Mark'ſt the world in buſtling ſhow,
Struggling o'er the waves of woe ;
By the wind of black deſpair,
Daſh'd away from care to care,
Whilſt thou, calm on Safety's ſhore,
Doſt but hear the tempeſt roar.
What if thou the flow'ry pride,
Of the meadow's velvet ſide,
To the proudly-arching bower,
And the glittering court of power,
Can'ſt prefer ; we envy not,
Holy Seer, thy ſimple lot.
Siſters twin are Youth and Pleaſure,
Mean't t'enjoy the ſweets of leiſure,
Made for every blithſome ſport,
Purpoſe mild, and gay reſort.
Age was form'd for meditation,
Not the toys of recreation,
With the ſmiles of Wiſdom fraught,
And the glow of ſolemn thought ;
Such is Age, Philoſophy,
Such the mind that ſuits with thee.

But now joys of different kind,
Wing the wiſh, and fire the mind ;

Tumbling

Tumbling rills that warbling flow,
Yellow meads with gold that glow,
Wandering walks, and rural eafe,
Such alone have power to pleafe.
Or perchance the lucid fcene,
Where the rays of Beauty's mien,
Kindling every fond defire,
Set the foul of Love on fire :
Or the loudly-echoing horn,
As it cheers the flumbering Morn,
Waking Nature, haply may
Lure us to the chace away.

Farewel then, thou willow'd ftream,
Glittering bright with Wifdom's beam,
Silver Cam ! whofe bowers among,
Infpiration leads her throng,
Clio breathes celeftial fire,
Mufic hangs her dulcet lyre,
Yet farewel !—to brighter joys,
Pleafure lifts our wandering eyes,
With her own refiftlefs fmile,
She fhall fmooth each care awhile;
Yes, fhe, fair Queen, fhall all the mind poffefs,
With gladnefs fire it, and with rapture blefs.

A N

AN EPITAPH

IN A COUNTRY CHURCH-YARD IN KENT.

BY MR. GRAY.

(AUTHOR OF THE ELEGY IN A COUNTRY CHURCH-YARD).

[Not printed in Johnſon's Edition of the Engliſh Poets.]

LO! where this ſilent marble weeps,
A friend, a wife, a mother ſleeps,
A heart, within whoſe ſacred cell
The peaceful virtues lov'd to dwell:
Affection warm, and faith ſincere,
And ſoft humanity were there.
In agony, in death reſign'd,
She felt the wound ſhe left behind:
Her infant image here below,
Sits ſmiling on a father's woe:
Whom what awaits, while thus he ſtrays
Along the lonely vale of days ?
A pang, to ſecret Sorrow dear,
A ſigh, an unavailing tear,
Till Time ſhall every grief remove,
With life, with memory, and with love.

N 5   DIA-

DIALOGUE BETWEEN CUPID AND HYMEN.

BY SIR JOHN VANBURGH.

CUPID.

THOU bane to my empire, thou spring of contest,
Thou source of all discord, thou foe to my rest,
Pray tell me what wretches in bondage can see,
That the aim of their life is directed to thee?

HYMEN.

Then tell me, thou little impertinent God,
Why the slaves of thy power, so afraid of thy nod,
Grow fond of a change, to whatever it be,
And I'll tell thee, why those would be bound who
  are free?

CUPID.

Were Love the reward of a pains-taking life,
Had a spouse the address to be fond of his wife,
Was Virtue so plenty, that a wife could afford,
In these very bad times, to be true to her Lord;
Some specious account might be given of all those,
Who are tied by the tail to be led by the nose.

        - But

But fince 'tis the fate of the wedded for life,
(Excepted a few) to love conteft and ftrife,
I think 'twere much wifer to ramble at large,
And the vollies of Love on the herd to difcharge.

HYMEN.

Was I but a Monarch fo cruelly juft,
To oblige a poor fpoufe to be true to his truft,
Some colour of reafon thy dictates might bear,
If a man had no more than a wife to his fhare;
But I never pretended, for many years paft,
By wedding young people to make 'em more chafte;
I therefore advife thee to let me go on,
Thou'lt find I'm the ftrength and fupport of thy
      throne;
For had'ft thou but eyes, thou would'ft quickly per-
      ceive it,
    How fmoothly thy dart
    Slips into the heart
    Of a woman that's wed,
    While the timorous maid
    Of thy arrow afraid,
    Flies the amorous bed,
While trembling, tho' wifhing, fhe dares not receive it.

N 6   ON.

ON CELIA's SICKNESS.

BY ISAAC HAWKINS BROWNE, ESQ.

[Not in the Volume of his Poems.]

CRUEL difeafe, thus to invade
The fhrine for Love and Graces made;
Can fhe to ficknefs be a prey,
Whofe charms made all the world look gay;
All but myfelf, whom lucklefs Fate
Ordains the victim of her hate:
I, wretched I! muft hourly mourn
The rigour of relentlefs fcorn.
Yet Celia's illnefs wounds me more
Than her fevere difdain before:
And, cruel! tho' fhe flights my pain,
Deaf as the winds when I complain,
Yet urg'd by generous paffions ftill,
Whate'er fhe fuffers I muft feel.
What tho' I cannot hope to fhare
The tender joys of life with her,
This privilege fhe can't refufe,
To be partaker in her woes.
But muft I then unpitied burn,
And never hope a kind return?
Obdurate in your firft intent,
Can nothing teach you to relent?

Oh!

Oh! could the ills which you fuftain,
Make you compaffionate my pain !
But yours are of a different kind,
Affect the body, not the mind.
Yours only reach the outward part,
Mine plant a dagger in my heart.

UPON READING THE LIFE OF THE JESUIT PREBER.

BY CAPTAIN THOMSON.

PREBER's great foul difdain'd what Fortune fent,
Amidft his foes imprifon'd found content.
Superior Virtue, happy in its ends,
Oft from our foes creates our beft of friends :
No fect or nation, native light the fame,
E'er gave to Vice fair Virtue's hallow'd name.
See with difdain exulting Vice abroad !
See at her heels flow Juftice with a rod !
Diff'rent with Virtue, modeft maid, whofe tears
Precede the many thoufand friends fhe rears.
Preber immur'd with Preber's dauntlefs breaft,
I'd rather chufe than Perfia's purple veft,
Beneath whofe gaudy folds the coward heart
Oft dreads, and juftly, the domeftic dart.

Princes,

Princes, whom love of fway, not Juftice lure,
Whom Flatt'rers poifon, but whom Patriots cure:
Look to the Eaft, fee arbitrary fway,
Thro' one dread tenor keep its ruthlefs way!
Nor Art or Science blefs the rolling years,
O'er hills of forrow, and through vales of tears;
The famifh'd hind, flow plodding on his way,
Scarce reaps in part the labours of the day:
In vain indulgent Nature fpreads her ftore,
While ev'ry petty tyrant robs the poor;
While gold, not Juftice, gives the faving pow'r,
While Vice itfelf's infur'd not for an hour.
Where Science fhone, now hoots the lonely owl,
Foxes obfcure, and hungry lions prowl;
Afia's fair.cities now in ruins laid,
And once her gardens, lonely deferts made;
All that was great or good, inverted ftand,
Now Blood, and Priefts, and Ignorance keep the land.
England's inftructed Monarch, learn from hence,
Your greateft glory, and your beft defence,
Confift in giving Liberty and Law:
Nor by ignoble Fear attempt to awe
Spirits who fcorn to wear the galling chain
Our neighbours wear--impoverifh'd France and Spain!
What fanguine floods for Liberty have run!
When Brutus ftruck—then Cæfar was undone.

HOR.

HOR. LIB. I. ODE XXII. IMITATED.

BY MISS ELIZABETH CARTER.

[Not in her Poems.]

Integer vitæ, &c.

A Virtuous man, whofe acts and thoughts are pure,
Without the help of weapons is fecure,
Without or quiver, or impoifon'd fpear,
His ftedfaft foul forgets the fenfe of fear.
Whether thro' Lybia's burning fands he goes,
Or Caucafe horrid with perpetual fnows ;
Surveys thofe regions where Hydafpes ftrays,
Or toft by tempefts in the raging feas ;
Safe in his own intrinfic worth remains,
And, arm'd with that, each obftacle difdains ;
Toils, dangers, difficulties all defied,
His paffport Virtue, Providence his guide.

If plac'd by Fate beneath the torrid zone,
Scorch'd by the fury of too near a Sun ;
Or fent where never Phœbus' cheerful ray,
Glad the dark climate with one glimpfe of day ;
Where no gay verdure decks th' unfruitful ground,
But Winter fpreads its empire all around :

Amidft.

Amidſt the terrors of that diſmal ſcene,
His mind preſerves a ſettled calm within.
To him the gloomy waſte ſhall ſeem to ſmile,
And conſcious Virtue ev'ry care beguile.
Virtue alike its tenor can maintain,
In ſplendid courts, or on a barren plain.

Diffugere Nives, redeunt jam Gramina Campis, &c.

HOR. L. IV. ODE VII. A TRANSLATION.

BY THE SAME.

[Not in her Poems.]

NOW Nature quickens with the vernal breeze,
Again their leafy honours deck the trees.
The ſmiling Earth renews her blooming pride,
And leſs'ning ſtreams within their channels glide.
The Nymphs and Graces on the plains advance,
And in gay circles lead the ſprightly dance.
The various changes of the ſeaſons ſhow,
That nought immortal muſt be hop'd below:
The ſwift-wing'd hours this ſerious truth convey,
Whoſe rapid motion hurries on the day.
The flow'ry Spring bids bluſt'ring tempeſts ceaſe,
To Summer's reign the flow'ry Spring gives place;
That too muſt fly when Autumn yields her ſtore,
And Winter next reſume its gloomy pow'r.

Yet

Yet as the Moon renews her filver horn,
Each dormant feafon fhall to life return.
But we, when deftin'd to that darkfome place,
From which nor Tullus' wealth, nor Ancus' race,
Nor e'en Æneas' piety could free,
Are nought but fleeting air, and lifelefs clay.
Who knows if Heav'n will add to morrow's Sun,
To crown thofe minutes we've already run?
Then each delight to footh thy mind prepare;
What's fpent in this, fhall 'fcape a greedy heir.
When Fate has once confign'd thee to the tomb,
And the ftern Judge pronounc'd thy final doom,
Nor Wit, Defcent, nor Piety can aid,
To refcue thee from Death's eternal fhade.
For neither can the Goddefs of the Wood,
Free her chafte favourite from the Stygian blood;
Nor Thefus (all his valiant efforts vain)
Releafe Pirithous from th' infernal chain.

A RIDDLE. BY THE SAME.

[Not in her Poems.]

NOR form, nor fubftance in my being fhare,
I'm neither fire, nor water, earth, nor air;
From motion's force alone my birth derive;
I ne'er can die, for never was alive:

And

And yet with such extensive empire reign,
That very few escape my magic chain.
Nor time, nor place, my wild excursions bound ;
I break all order, Nature's laws confound : .
Raise schemes without contrivance or design,
And make apparent contradictions join ;
Transfer the Thames where Ganges waters roll,
Unite 'th' Equator to the frozen pole ;
Mid'st Zembla's ice bid blushing rubies glow,
And British harvests bloom in Scythian snow ;
Cause trembling flocks to skim the raging main,
And scaly fishes graze the verdant plain ;
Make light descend, and heavy bodies rise,
Stars sink to earth, and earth ascend to skies.
If Nature lie deform'd in Wint'ry frost,
And all the beauties of the Spring be lost,
Rais'd by my pow'r, new verdure decks the ground,
And smiling flow'rs diffuse their sweets around.
The sleeping dead I summon from the tomb,
And oft anticipate the living's doom ;
Convey offenders to the fatal tree,
When law or stratagem have set them free.
Aw'd by no checks my roving flights can soar
Beyond Imagination's active pow'r.
I view each country of the spacious earth,
Nay, visit realms that never yet had birth ;
Can trace the pathless regions of the air,
And fly, with ease, beyond the starry sphere.

So

So fwift my operations, in an hour
I can deſtroy a town, or build a tow'r;
Play tricks would puzzle all the ſearch of Wit,
And ſhew whole volumes that were never writ.
In ſure records my myſtic pow'rs confeſt,
Who rack'd with cares a haughty tyrant's breaſt;
Charg'd in prophetic emblems to relate
Approaching wrath, and his peculiar fate.
Oft to the good by Heaven in Mercy ſent,
I've arm'd their thoughts againſt ſome dire event;
As oft in chains preſumptuous villains bind,
And haunt with reſtleſs fears the guilty mind.

Nullum Numen habes ſi ſit Prudentia, ſed te
Nos facimus, Fortuna, Deam, Cœloque locamus.

JUV.

BY THE SAME.

[Not in her Poems.]

WHATEVER we think on't, Fortune's but a toy,
Which cheats the ſoul with empty ſhows of joy;
A meer ideal creature of the brain,
That reigns the idol of the mad and vain;
Deludes their ſenſes with a fair diſguiſe,
And ſets an airy bliſs before their eyes.

But

But when they hope to grasp the glitt'ring prey,
Th' instable phantom vanishes away.

So vap'ry fires mislead unwary swains,
Who rove benighted o'er the dewy plains.
Drawn by the faithless meteor's glimm'ring ray,
Thro' devious paths, and lonely wilds they stray !
Too late convinc'd their sad mistake deplore,
And find their home more distant than before.

Could mortals learn to limit their desires,
Little supplies what Nature's want requires ;
Content affords an inexhausted store,
And void of that a Monarch's wealth is poor.

Grant but ten thousand pounds, Plilaurus cries,
That happy sum would all my wants suffice.
Assenting pow'rs the golden blessing grant,
But with his wealth his wishes too augment.
With anxious care he pines amidst his store,
And starves himself to get ten thousand more.

Ambition's charms Philotimus inspire,
A Treas'rer's staff the pitch of his desire:
The staff he gains, yet murmurs at his fate,
And longs to shine first Minister of State.

A coach and four employ'd Cosmelia's cares,
For this she hourly worried Heav'n with pray'rs.

Did

Did this, when gain'd, her reſtleſs temper fix ?
No, ſhe ſtill prays—For what ?—A coach and ſix.

Thus when thro' Fortune's airy rounds we ſtray,
Our footſteps rove from Nature's certain way ;
Thro' endleſs labyrinth of Error run,
And by the fond deluſion are undone ;
Still vainly reaching at a tranſient bliſs,
Purſue the ſhadow, and the ſubſtance miſs:
Till after all our wand'ring ſchemes, we find
That true content dwells only in the mind.
Thoſe joys on no external aid depend,
But in ourſelves begin, and there muſt end.
From Virtue only thoſe delights muſt flow,
Which neither wealth nor titles can beſtow.

A ſoul, which uncorrupted Reaſon ſways,
With calm indiff'rence Fortune's gifts ſurveys.
If Providence an affluent ſtore denies,
Its own intrinſic worth that want ſupplies ;
Diſdains by vicious actions to acquire
That glitt'ring trifle vulgar minds admire.
With eaſe to Heav'n's ſuperior will reſigns,
Nor meanly at another's wealth repines.
Firmly adheres to Virtue's ſteady rules,
And ſcorns the fickle deity of fools.

IN

IN DIEM NATALEM.

Εκ Διος αρχωμεσθα, και εις Δια ληγετε, Μοισας.
THEOC.

——*Vivendi recte qui prorogat Horam*
Rusticus expectat dum defluat Amnis ; at ille
Labitur, & labetur in omne volubilis Ævum. HORAT.

· [This is in her Works, but much altered.]

THOU power fupreme, by whofe command I live,
The grateful tribute of my praife receive,
To thy indulgence I my being owe,
And all the joys which from that being flow.
Scarce eighteen funs have form'd the rolling year,
And run their deftin'd courfes round this fphere,
Since thou my undiftinguifh'd frame furvey'd,
Among the lifelefs heaps of matter laid.
Thy fkill my elemental clay refin'd,
The ftraggling parts in beauteous order join'd,
With perfect fymmetry compos'd the whole,
And ftampt thy facred image on my foul ;
A foul fufceptible of endlefs joy,
Whofe frame, nor force, nor time, can e'er deftroy,
But fhall fubfift when Nature claims my breath,
And bid defiance to the pow'r of death ;
To realms of blifs with active Freedom foar,
And live when earth and fkies fhall be no more.

Indu'gent

Indulgent God ! in vain my tongue eſſays,
For this immortal gift, to ſpeak thy praiſe.
How ſhall my heart its grateful ſenſe reveal,
Where all the energy of words muſt fail?
O may its influence in my life appear,
And every action prove my thanks ſincere !

Grant me, great God, a heart to thee inclin'd;
Increaſe my faith, and rectify my mind.
Teach me betimes to tread thy ſacred ways,
And to thy ſervice conſecrate my days,
Still as thro' Life's uncertain maze I ſtray,
Be thou the guiding ſtar to mark my way.
Conduct the ſteps of my unguarded youth,
And point their motions to the paths of Truth.
Protect me by thy providential care,
And teach my ſoul t' avoid the tempter's ſnare.
Thro' all the varied ſcenes of human life,
In calms of eaſe, or bluſt'ring ſtorms of grief;
Thro' every turn of this inconſtant ſtate,
Preſerve my temper equal and ſedate.
Give me a mind that bravely dares deſpiſe
The low deſigns and artifice of Vice.
Be my religion ſuch as taught by thee,
Alike from Pride and Superſtition free.
Inform my judgment, rectify my will,
Confirm my reaſon, and my paſſions ſtill.

To

To gain thy favour be my only end,
And to that scope my every action tend.
Amidst the pleasures of a prosp'rous state,
Whose flatt'ring charms too oft the mind elate,
Still may I think to whom those joys I owe,
And bless the bounteous hand from whence they flow.
Or if an adverse fortune be my share,
Let not its terrors tempt me to despair;
But bravely arm'd a steady faith maintain,
And own all best which thy decrees ordain;
On thy almighty providence depend,
The best protector, and the surest friend.

Thus on Life's stage may I my part maintain,
And at my exit thy applauses gain.

F I N I S.

Lightning Source UK Ltd.
Milton Keynes UK
UKOW012138101212

203464UK00009B/702/P